Building Your CareerPortfolio

By

Carol A. Poore

CAREER PRESS
FRANKLIN LAKES, NJ

BUILDING YOUR CAREERPORTFOLIO
Cover design by Fanzone Design Solutions
Edited by Karen Prager
Typeset by Eileen Munson
Printed in the U.S.A. by Book-mart Press

To order this title, please call toll-free 1-800-CAREER-1 (NJ and Canada: 201-848-0310) to order using VISA or MasterCard, or for further information on books from Career Press.

CAREER
PRESS

The Career Press, Inc., 3 Tice Road, PO Box 687,
Franklin Lakes, NJ 07417
www.careerpress.com

Library of Congress Cataloging-in-Publication Data

Poore, Carol A.
    Building your careerportfolio / by Carol A. Poore
        p. cm.
    Includes index.
    ISBN 1-56414-540-9 (paper)
        1. Career development. I. Title.

HF5381 .P664 2001
650.14—dc21

00-065107

Disclaimer

Dedication

*This book is dedicated
to you, the reader
who seeks
to live each day
with purpose.*

Acknowledgments...

I'm thankful for the many people and experiences that have shaped my career journey and inspired this book. In particular, I thank my mother and father, Mary Lou and Edgar F. White, for their nurturing love, faith, and encouragement to pursue my dreams. As a result, I was able to develop the beginnings of a CareerPortfolio during my childhood and to define the concept as an adult.

I thank my husband, David, and sons, Justin and Nathan, for their patience and encouragement during the years I researched and wrote this book. I thank those involved in the hundreds of interviews and focus groups I conducted, as well as my colleagues who provided inspiration along the way. Many thanks to my editors, Jodi Decker and the team from Career Press, especially Karen Prager.

I also recognize Salt River Project, where I developed both executive and community leadership skills within a corporate setting. This century-old water and power company in Arizona demonstrates its rich, pioneering heritage of responsibility and servant leadership by generously encouraging its people to make a difference in the communities where customers are served. Salt River Project and its people will always be near and dear to my heart.

Mission Statement...

This book is designed to help each reader develop a dynamic CareerPortfolio of wise career investments—investments that pay off in the ability to fulfill a personal purpose and navigate lifelong career transitions. CareerPortfolio is a pending trademark of Carol A. Poore.

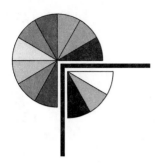

Table of Contents

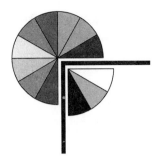

Introduction

What would it take for you to find meaning and personal reward in your life's work? How could you begin to develop a simplified way to fulfill your hopes and dreams in the work that you do each and every day? What would it take to feel excited about going to work each day?

The answer is: purpose. And, making purposeful career investments. I want you to think of your personal purpose as your own, personal career DNA that unlocks the rich and meaningful career investments that will help you grow—personally and professionally—throughout your changing lifetime. Your personal purpose is unique to you, and to you alone.

In my parents' day, work wasn't personal, and it wasn't supposed to be fun. Today, all of that has changed. Work is not about submerging our identity—it's about finding it and leveraging it so that we can find meaning and new choices as we move forward in life. Not only do we crave work that's fun, we want to learn, grow, and make a difference in the world in which we live.

If you're searching for a greater sense of career purpose, you may be:

➤ Tired of grinding away at endless projects—but yearning for a more purposeful, meaningful career.

➤ Looking for practical ways to *proactively* prepare for career and life change.

➤ Searching for a simpler way to make a difference in your world.

➤ Worried about your skills or your job becoming obsolete.

If you answered yes to any of the statements above, then this book is for you. My trademarked CareerPortfolio system provides a new way of approaching your career. It is an approach that helps you view your career as a *whole lifetime of meaningful investments*, rather than just the job or business you own today. The CareerPortfolio is a diversified "investment portfolio" of four career investments that can help you achieve big dividends, or personal rewards, over time. Guided by a defined personal purpose, you will be able to cut to the chase when it comes to making career investments.

Instead of feeling frustrated and trapped by your job or current situation, you will gain a practical way to position yourself for new career options and opportunities. And, you will never, ever want to put all of your career eggs in one basket (in other words, your job) again!

We'll explore the four CareerPortfolio investments:

1. Primary Income Investment.

2. Secondary Income Investment.

3. Volunteer Income Investment.

4. Lifelong Learning Investment.

These career investments are relevant at any stage of life:

In your twenties—   as you sharpen your work habits and seek ways to build your personal credibility.

In your career-building stage—
when you build momentum as a leader and decision maker.

In your mid-life years— when people often desire new pursuits. (For some, this could mean a return to the workplace after raising children.)

In your latter years— as you desire to remain active and productive, using your career nest egg as a springboard for meaningful daily life.

Why are steady and *purposeful* career investments important? Because, bottom line, you will need to be change oriented throughout the rest of your life. You will need a way to cut through the clutter and noise of everyday life in order to decide which career-related activities are valuable.

You may be among the 124 million baby boomers and post-boomers who are moving toward the second half of their careers, contemplating the quality of life and wanting to ensure that every moment spent on the job is spent in a way that adds purpose to their lives. And, you will be working with younger, "Generation Y-ers" who will be your employees and colleagues.

> ➤ You're likely to change professions (fields of study) three times in your life.

> ➤ You can count on the fact that every two to five years, you're likely to make a change. You might find a different job, pursue a new field of work, reduce your work hours, or sell a business you own or have inherited. Few of us can realistically plan to stay within one organization for longer than five years.

> ➤ You'll probably be living longer and working more years than those in generations past. (The average life span has grown from 65 in 1935 to 75 today.)

> ➤ In today's knowledge-based society, you must be flexible to respond quickly to an opportunity in order to implement change. Competitive advantage is not simply innovation—it takes flexible people to implement the innovation. Your CareerPortfolio can help you become more flexible as you build career investments and think of change as a normal and positive part of living.

This book is unique because it's not about job interviews and resumes. Instead, *Building Your CareerPortfolio* is designed to:

1. Help you discover your personal (and professional) purpose.

2. Help you plan a combination of career investments that can help you build "career wealth" over time. The approach is similar to the way a financial investor builds a financial portfolio of assets. With a directed approach to building specific investments, you can achieve a more purposeful career and be prepared to face constant change in the new millennium.

In addition to the four career investments, *Building Your Career-Portfolio* features:

> ➤ Real examples of purposeful people who are taking a CareerPortfolio approach.

> ➤ Personal journals in each chapter, where you can plan tangible steps to implement your CareerPortfolio ideas.

> ➤ Appendices filled with additional tips and valuable resources.

Building Your CareerPortfolio will be a resource that you can read now and refer back to throughout your lifetime. Each chapter can be read as a stand-alone resource depending on your needs and priorities.

Your career is a huge life investment. Chances are, you'll spend more than half of your life working in a career-related capacity. You can make every investment of time and energy count! I urge you to reap a purposeful future as you plan and grow your portfolio of career assets, your CareerPortfolio.

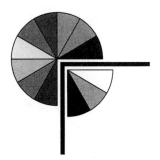

Chapter 1

The CareerPortfolio

You've heard the saying: "The job belongs to the company." (Subtext: Your job could be here today and gone tomorrow.) If you are job-focused rather than career-focused, you may eventually become a passenger on your career journey instead of the driver.

There is good news, however. Your *career* belongs to *you*. And, in this historic time, when most of us are trying to focus and simplify our busy, hurried lives, we search for tools to help us make the very best time investments possible. The CareerPortfolio is designed to help you find greater focus in your career life, along with investments that help you minimize career risk and maximize personal rewards and purpose.

After all, your career is a "portfolio" of valuable investments that no one can ever take from you. Consider these insights from career gurus.

"Your career is an evolution of experiences that prepare you to
earn current *and future* income."

—Michael Hammer, re-engineering expert

"A career is technically *your total life* in the world of work."

—Richard Nelson Bolles, author, *What Color Is Your Parachute?*

"Your career is your life work in fulfilling a purpose."

—Joanne Hawes, president and founder of
Life Purpose International

Best-selling author Charles Handy saw life as a diversified portfolio. In his renowned book, *The Age of Unreason*, Handy masterfully describes life as a collection of different parts, with the whole being greater than the sum of the parts. Handy's view of the career-related portfolio includes paid work, homework (tasks in the home that must be done), gift work (volunteering), and study work (learning). He believes the most difficult but needed transition of the future is to move from the lifestyle of wage work, where one's career equals his or her job, to the pursuit of a portfolio career, where each area is represented.

Handy believes that "portfolio lives" include the ability to:

➤ Control what you do.

➤ Use knowledge and experience to make decisions.

➤ Have a variety of things to do throughout one's lifetime.

You can take a portfolio approach to your career, too. Nothing illustrates a diversified career better than understanding how a financial portfolio works. You can apply the same investment principles found in building a financial portfolio to growing what I call "career wealth."

CareerPortfolio:
Similar to a financial portfolio

A financial portfolio is a combination of financial assets (see Figure 1). Besides cash, financial portfolios often contain stock, bonds, parcels of real estate, or other assets that an investor owns. The idea of diversifying risk means that you would want to select a number of investment assets so that if one asset is performing poorly, another asset will be performing well. You would achieve what we call a "hedge" in finance. (Chapter 2 describes career risk.)

➤ Different types of financial investment opportunities differ in their potential for return on investment, as well as in the risk of either earning money or losing money. In the investment world, typically, the greater the desired return, the greater the risk that must be assumed by you, the investor. Risk, in turn, is controlled through diversification.

➤ Financial experts advocate that the most important thing in accumulating financial wealth is to say no to uncontrolled spending. This is an important rule that applies to building career wealth! You must be able to say no to uncontrolled or random spending of your time, energy, and talent in order to be free to say yes to wise career investments.

➤ No single investment is right for everyone. Everyone invests for the same basic reason: to make assets work synergistically to meet a set of objectives. Your unique financial needs, desires, and circumstances determine which specific investments are appropriate for your situation.

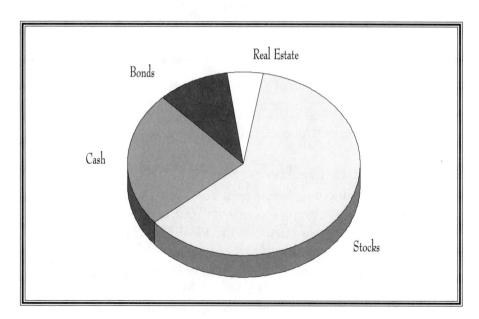

Figure 1: Example of a financial portfolio

CareerPortfolio: A practical model

The CareerPortfolio is a model of four important career "assets." The four investments offer a well-balanced opportunity for you to earn, learn, and help others (see Figure 2).

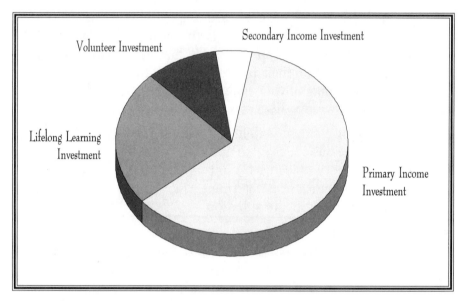

Figure 2: Example of a CareerPortfolio

The four CareerPortfolio assets are:

1. Primary Income Investment

Your Primary Income Investment represents your largest career focus, whether you are employed or own your own business. Whether it's your job, or your own business, the ideal Primary Income Investment is meaningful and enjoyable.

⇒ **Financial parallel:** Your Primary Income Investment is much like investing in a blue chip stock or mutual fund composed of blue chip stocks. These are stocks of the world's largest and most financially sound companies, which typically provide steady growth and dividend income.

2. Secondary Income Investment

Whether you are employed or own your own business, adding a Secondary Income Investment to your CareerPortfolio is an excellent way to learn new skills, create career options, and earn extra income in the process. This is an alternate source of income that *you* control. It is *not* a second job working for someone else. It could be an annual project, a financial investment that you manage, or a hobby that provides you with an alternate income source, such as singing at weddings. If you own a business, it could mean diversifying your business into separate functions or product lines.

⇒ **Financial parallel:** Your Secondary Income Investment is similar to investing in a higher-risk stock. Higher-risk stocks, under the right circumstances, may earn greater returns than lower-risk investments, but are less consistent or predictable than blue chip stocks. In like manner, your Secondary Income Investment, over time, could yield bigger monetary rewards as well as greater personal satisfaction than your current Primary Income Investment. In the investment world, higher-risk stocks are not meant to provide primary investment return, but to allow above-average growth. Your Secondary Income Investment may provide additional learning experiences that far surpass the professional growth possible in your Primary Income Investment.

3. Volunteer Investment, or giving to others

Volunteer Investments can provide you with opportunities to develop new skills, meet community leaders, and contribute your talents to benefit others. Volunteers are likely to be dedicated employees with superior leadership skills. In Chapter 6, you will learn valuable tips about selecting the right Volunteer Investment to match your personal purpose.

⇒ **Financial parallel:** Volunteering your time and mental focus is similar to investing money in bonds. Bonds are lower-risk investment vehicles compared to stocks, and the return on investment grows over a longer period of time. Consider your volunteering as an investment similar to bonds in a financial portfolio. A bond is a long-term investment strategy. It's a loan for the return of the principal plus interest. With volunteerism, you are "loaning" your expertise and time in return for new experiences not found in your current duties. Volunteer Investments are not a get-rich-quick strategy. With steady Volunteer Investments, your career wealth and opportunities will grow steadily over time.

4. Lifelong Learning Investments

There are three specific Lifelong Learning Investments that can help you grow your career wealth:

➤ **Focused reading**—emphasizing your purpose, your field, new technology valuable to your job, personal finances, and positive thinking.

➤ **Focused education**—training, workshops, classes, and advanced degrees pursued throughout your life.

➤ **Mentorship**— both having and being a mentor and using personal think tanks and boards of directors.

We'll explore these Lifelong Learning Investments in Chapter 7.

⇒ **Financial parallel:** Lifelong Learning Investments are similar to cash. Cash is highly liquid and is used on the spot when needed. Your Lifelong Learning Investments are easy to deploy and can be immediately applied to most any career and life situation. It's important to note that cash does not withstand the negative impact of inflation unless invested wisely. In like manner, if you do not put your Lifelong Learning to work for you, these tools may become obsolete over time.

By developing *at least two of the four career assets* in your CareerPortfolio, you'll be better equipped to make changes that support your purpose in life. Your unique variety of career assets will serve as a springboard for new options and opportunities.

The key is to select the appropriate mix of investments that help you earn the *highest returns on your investments over time*. That means you'll want to make investments that support your evolving purpose and priorities (we'll get to that in Chapter 3). You can make each career investment work as hard as possible for you, to help you minimize risk and maximize a purposeful and fulfilling life.

For example, meet Joyce, a single mother of two boys. Here's how she applied a low-risk CareerPortfolio strategy during a major life turning point.

Joyce, the Green Thumb

Joyce, who loved to garden, was thrust into a career-building mode when her life was turned upside down on the heels of a divorce. Joyce had two kids and no job. What would she do to make ends meet after being a stay-at-home mom for many years?

"I considered my options. Without a college degree, working for someone else was not a financially viable choice due to low-paying wages and high child-care costs," she said.

As a Primary Income Investment, she fell back on her lifetime hobby of growing plants and arranging flowers. As friends would purchase plants from Joyce's hobby garden, she discovered that her best income opportunity could be as close as her backyard.

"As a kid I loved working outdoors, picking strawberries and vegetables," she recalled. "It was fun to be a part of things that grow—and turn this into a business of my own."

With meager funds left from the divorce, Joyce purchased a small house on a state highway intersection in central Maine. With help from family, she built her first greenhouse in her backyard.

"I knew the greenhouse wouldn't sustain our living expenses, so I also sold homemade gifts such as wreaths, teddy bears, dolls, and quilts," she said. "This became my Secondary Income Investment. During the first few years I worked seven days a week, taking care of the plants and getting the store ready for the next week."

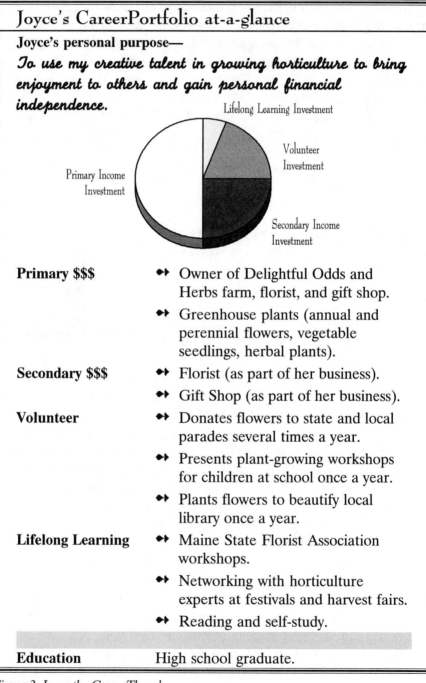

Joyce's CareerPortfolio at-a-glance

Joyce's personal purpose—

To use my creative talent in growing horticulture to bring enjoyment to others and gain personal financial independence.

Primary $$$	➳ Owner of Delightful Odds and Herbs farm, florist, and gift shop.
	➳ Greenhouse plants (annual and perennial flowers, vegetable seedlings, herbal plants).
Secondary $$$	➳ Florist (as part of her business).
	➳ Gift Shop (as part of her business).
Volunteer	➳ Donates flowers to state and local parades several times a year.
	➳ Presents plant-growing workshops for children at school once a year.
	➳ Plants flowers to beautify local library once a year.
Lifelong Learning	➳ Maine State Florist Association workshops.
	➳ Networking with horticulture experts at festivals and harvest fairs.
	➳ Reading and self-study.
Education	High school graduate.

Figure 3: Joyce the Green Thumb

Joyce sold crafts made by local residents as well as her own handmade gifts, which brought year-round business into the store. As the business developed, Joyce was able to focus more effort on supporting community events and taking classes. She donated flower arrangements to local city parades and presented school workshops. These occasional Volunteer Investments added to Joyce's commitment to her community. As an added benefit, she nearly doubled her store's business—her volunteer work resulted in greater business volume as well as new business contacts.

For Lifelong Learning Investments, Joyce attends harvest fairs and workshops where her field is discussed. She looks forward to these inexpensive, "share and compare" sessions that bring fresh ideas to her business.

"The best part is that I don't have to financially depend on anyone else with this diversified business approach. I've learned how to adjust my living expenses to the inflow of sales. I'm able to direct my own schedule to make it happen," she says.

Making Her CareerPortfolio Work

- Joyce was determined to integrate her business startup with raising her two boys as a single mom.
- She was able to enlist some help from family members, which maximized her available time and provided a good source of encouragement.
- Her parents pitched in as helpers during the first few years. As her boys grew older, they became involved with the gardening and chores.
- By having her business attached to her home, Joyce saved travel time and kept her costs down. She couldn't afford to purchase or rent a separate store, and with two young boys, she needed the flexibility that a cottage industry could provide.

What happens when you are thrust into the role of supporting yourself for the first time in your life? The first step is to find the best possible Primary Income Investment that supports your personal purpose. Like starting a financial investment plan, your first career investment should be made with the idea that it may some day help you fund a diversified CareerPortfolio. Ask the question, "How will my Primary Income Investment help support my ability to diversify my career at another time?" Over time, you can begin to cultivate other career assets.

How Does Joyce Do It?

Monday	Tuesday	Wednesday	Thursday	Friday	Saturday	Sunday
Full-time work 8 a.m. to 6 p.m. Monday - Saturday at home-based greenhouse						
and floral/gift shop. (Primary and Secondary Investments.)						Family Time
Volunteering a couple of hours during occasional business days.					Occasional harvest fairs and floral seminars: about once a quarter on a Saturday.	
Family Time						

Figure 4: Joyce's schedule

CareerPortfolio benefits: The payoffs

Here are the payoffs you can expect when you build a Career-Portfolio. Figure 5 provides a view of additional benefits.

➤ If you face a job or business loss, you can be flexible and tap into other career-related areas to sustain income and/or make immediate and productive changes.

➤ Your job may not always provide you with a high level of satisfaction, but other career-building investments provide personal fulfillment and help to balance times of dissatisfaction.

➤ You gain new business referrals through your other career-related investments. The diversity of projects can help you build teamwork skills as you partner with others.

➤ You'll start by clearly defining your personal purpose; this will provide focus throughout your lifetime.

➤ You can maximize your ability to learn, earn, and help others.

Benefits of the CareerPortfolio

The ability to simply retain a job.

A purposeful mind-set, or attitude, geared toward the future.

A tool for developing personal purpose and a hedge against career risk.

Meaningful business contacts and friendships.

Contentment with your ability to be a contributor.

The ability to start and grow your own business.

A unique balance of helping yourself, and personal reward from helping others.

Professional advice from peers and mentors, of which you wouldn't otherwise have access.

Upward mobility; the ability to get promoted.

A financial safety net in the event you lose your primary job or business.

Opportunities to learn, stay on the cutting edge of new trends, and become more experienced in your field.

A better ability to switch careers and try something similar, somewhat different, or entirely new.

Figure 5: Benefits of the CareerPortfolio

You, the business owner

If you own your own business, your CareerPortfolio will greatly enhance your personal range of experiences over time. You can use this tool to help your employees develop their skills, too. Additionally, you can use the CareerPortfolio as a tool for reinforcing your company's commitment to the community. In the process, you can develop important business relationships vital to your business. Consider how the following CareerPortfolio concepts can help your employees thrive.

Primary Investment: You can provide a number of incentives to keep your employees excited about their Primary Income Source. An attractive workplace and flexible hours are two examples. You encourage your employees to look at new opportunities for growth at your company.

Secondary Investment: Recognize that for those employees who can balance additional projects, running their own businesses may help them develop additional business expertise (as long as they're not running their business on your company time!). These people often are creative, highly motivated, and likely to be entrepreneurial in nature.

Volunteerism: You can encourage volunteer board and professional association involvement. If appropriate, you can provide a certain amount of time for volunteerism during the work day.

Lifelong Learning Investments: You can help your employees discover and attend enrichment courses. You might consider offering a tuition reimbursement program. You can return from seminars and workshops and bring a set of notes for your staff.

> ## Three steps to developing CareerPortfolio investments:
>
> **Step 1:** **Develop your investment strategy** (your personal purpose statement). Keep in mind your life stage (time horizon) and tolerance for risk. You can determine your career investment profile by completing the CareerPortfolio Investment Profile in Appendix A.
>
> **Step 2:** **Select the right career investments** to support your personal purpose.
>
> **Step 3:** **Monitor your career investments** on a regular basis, and update your CareerPortfolio when needed.

Making CareerPortfolio time

Your investments of time and mental focus (effort) are precious resources that you can control in a changing world that you cannot control. Your CareerPortfolio will help you focus the time that you set aside to achieve work-related pursuits.

The CareerPortfolio is not designed to drain time away from your family or needed relaxation. Rather, it's a model for helping you think about and plan your career-focused efforts. You may be able to scale down your Primary Income Investment time to find the extra hours for other career investments. Finding and making time will be something you'll have to force yourself to do if you're a workaholic. If you cannot scale back your Primary Income Investment time, you'll need to use your existing time more wisely to accommodate new career investments. Perhaps you can watch less television or eliminate activities not related to your personal purpose (see Chapter 3).

Let's say you currently invest a minimum of 45 career-related hours into your Primary Income Investment each week. Rather than invest all 45 hours in your Primary Income Investment, you may choose to spend at least five hours per week on other career assets, shown in Figure 6.

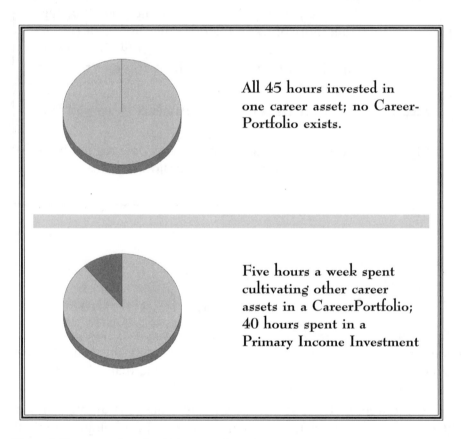

All 45 hours invested in one career asset; no Career-Portfolio exists.

Five hours a week spent cultivating other career assets in a CareerPortfolio; 40 hours spent in a Primary Income Investment

Figure 6: Two examples of a 45-hour work week

This concept can be adapted to fit a part-time worker's situation as well. If you work part time, you may decide to spend 20 hours per week focusing on your Primary Income Investment and find five hours per week for other career investments.

Personal Journal...
Draw Your CareerPortfolio

How do you spend your career-related time? Draw your current CareerPortfolio.

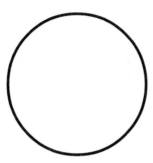

Now draw your desired CareerPortfolio.

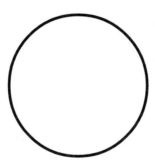

An additional CareerPortfolio Goals and Action Plan worksheet is included in Appendix B.

Chapter 2

Understanding
Career Risk

What, exactly, *is* career risk?

Career risk is anything that challenges your ability to work and find fulfillment in your life's work. Even if you are a dedicated employee and do everything right, career risk can happen when it's least expected. As one senior vice president said the day the bank eliminated his position: "I feel like used Kleenex."

There are three major types of career risk:

➤ Economic risk, such as mergers, acquisitions, bankruptcies, and layoffs.

➤ Company politics.

➤ Personal areas of risk, such as having obsolete skills, facing long-term illness, or acquiring a disability that affects your ability to work.

Most of the time there is little you can do to affect the first type of risk. Economic decisions are made across the globe each day to improve the bottom-line results of businesses. However, by working smart, keeping yourself healthy, and taking a diversified CareerPortfolio approach, you can do your part to mitigate the second and third types of risk while ensuring that you and your job add value to the business bottom line.

The latest career risk: becoming obsolete

Today's workforce must be ready to adapt to change driven by technology. In many cases, work that was performed by people is now automated and performed by computers. Becoming obsolete is one of the newest forms of career risk.

Obsolete workers tend to:

➤ Fail to update skills and seek new information to supplement their existing set of skills and knowledge base.

➤ Fail to see the warning signs of change.

➤ Fail to have a career back-up plan.

➤ Be disorganized in a job that requires new success habits.

➤ Be inflexible and fixed to what worked in the past.

➤ Produce just enough to get by, barely staying afloat.

➤ Isolate themselves from others rather than collaborate.

Personal Journal...

Reflection on obsolescence

Think of someone you know who once was successful but no longer is a contributor in his or her work environment. What happened to cause this person to become obsolete?

_____

_____

_____

_____

CareerPortfolio definitions

⇒ **Career crossroads:** Times of transition, when you sense that a change is in the works. Career transitions can be positive when you are ready to make the leap into something new.

⇒ **Career crisis:** Unexpected or shocking news that negatively affects your job or your career plans. (The objective of the CareerPortfolio is to help you avoid career crises.)

⇒ **Career risk:** Any situation or circumstance that may have a damaging effect on your ability to get hired, earn income, increase your relevancy in your work environment, receive promotions, and stay employed. (All of us are subject to some level of career risk.)

⇒ **Career wealth and career payoffs:** The ability to leverage or build new career options from your existing investments, even during times of career crises.

Getting the ax

Many devoted professionals have poured themselves into their jobs, working evenings and weekends. It's ironic that in many instances, they've been overlooked for promotions because they lacked the diversity of experiences that one gains from working in a variety of situations. With no backup plans, they are shocked when their jobs are eliminated. Look what happened to Phil.

The day that Phil got demoted, it might as well have been the ax.

Phil had put in hundreds of extra hours without pay as a public relations executive. He had worked his way into the hearts of upper management. He spent countless weekends and evenings in the office and on 24-hour call with the news media. Everyone admired Phil's tenacity—everyone except the new vice president, whom Phil had unintentionally upstaged at a corporate event. Phil was set up to make a swift exit with the boss's ultimatum: be demoted two levels downward, or leave the company with two months' severance pay.

Phil was shocked and devastated. He knew he couldn't stay and have his skills be underutilized in demoralizing circumstances.

Upon reflection, Phil realized his career mistakes. He had isolated himself from important career-building relationships. He had placed "face time" at the office and obsession with perfection before taking a break and making career investments now and then. His job became his identity. He was driven by his job instead of his personal purpose. He lacked alternate career plans, and was unsure what his skills were worth outside the company in which he worked. By devoting himself to his job, Phil banked on the fact that he was a permanent fixture.

It was nearly a year before Phil regrouped. He found a new job and developed a number of CareerPortfolio assets.

Perhaps you're a hard-working professional like Phil, who is so intent on doing a good job that personal purpose and meaning are totally lost. Your work life *and* family life are thrown off-balance as obsession with your job takes priority. Take heed of Phil's mistake: His options and relationships faded as he allowed a company to take first place in his life.

How Can You Mitigate Risk?

You can protect yourself against career risk by building a CareerPortfolio.

> ➤ Increase your job competency by offering superior knowledge and work habits (persistence, diligence, timeliness, character, etc.).

> ➤ Keep up-to-date by continually learning.

> ➤ Establish leadership skills and position yourself as someone who sets an example for others to follow.

> ➤ Develop connections in your community.

> ➤ Pursue other activities to fulfill your purpose in life (whether for pay or as a volunteer).

And remember:

> ➤ Job market risk never can be *completely* eliminated. In career terms, this means that all career decisions you'll ever make will feature both risks and trade-offs.

> ➤ As it is with a financial investor who has diversified investments, the investor who establishes a diversified CareerPortfolio knows that the total risk of a single investment is not critically important, because the investor is focused on the performance of the whole portfolio in marketplace conditions. You'll have a number of assets to "leverage," or put to use on your behalf.

Facing Career Crossroads

Career crossroads happen. It's not a matter of *if*. It's a matter of *when*. The following symptoms of stress are a normal part of career change. You may want to seek professional help if you find that these symptoms are causing you to lose self-control and a balanced perspective.

⇛ Anger.

⇛ Sadness and depression.

⇛ Inability to sleep as normal.

⇛ Inability to eat as normal.

⇛ Dread.

⇛ Feeling that you're all alone.

⇛ Inability to concentrate and complete job tasks; being preoccupied with circumstances that you may not be able to control.

When you are experiencing a major career transition, your CareerPortfolio will be useful for creating career options. It can be a great source of comfort, inspiration, and direction because you can draw from your various career assets to develop the most purposeful next steps.

Personal Journal...

Assessing Your Career Risk

1. Check the areas below for which you could be at risk in the next 12 months:

    ___ Layoffs.

    ___ Rumored layoffs (where behavior among peers, superiors, and subordinates often turns sour and, in some cases, rotten).

    ___ Your skills' becoming dull or even obsolete.

    ___ Personality conflicts.

    ___ Conflict between your values and ideals and those of the company.

    ___ Your age (being perceived as too old, too young, or as having been with the company too long).

    ___ Health risks.

    ___ Stress/burnout.

2. Check the statements that best describe your career.

    ___ My current job dominates all of my time. I'm swamped and need to find a way to build other important career investments.

    ___ I have drafted a personal purpose statement (vision or mission statement).

    ___ I have an alternate source of income that I control.

    ___ I am involved in a meaningful volunteer project.

    ___ I regularly update my learning through training, reading, and career-related advisement.

3. To assess your strategic career assets, describe the following:
   Your career strengths.

   _____

   _____

   _____

   _____

   Your career weaknesses.

   _____

   _____

   _____

   _____

   Your career opportunities.

   _____

   _____

   _____

   _____

   Your career threats.

   _____

   _____

   _____

   _____

By assessing your potential career risks, you're already better prepared to face change. Appendix B includes additional information to help you assess your time horizon and tolerance for risk. The first step to planning your CareerPortfolio, however, is to develop a keen sense of your unique, personal purpose. Chapter 3 will help you do exactly that.

Chapter 3

Personal Purpose: Your Investment Strategy

Your first step to developing a CareerPortfolio is to develop a personal purpose statement. This is similar to a business mission statement that describes what the business achieves. Your personal purpose is the *most significant* aspect of your CareerPortfolio, because it describes why you exist. It will become the driving force behind your plans. It will simplify your life, because you will be able to quickly determine if activities support your purpose, or if they detour, delay, or completely derail you from achieving your purpose.

Why is your personal purpose statement so important?

➤ Your personal purpose will help you develop fewer and more effective career investments.

➤ With your purpose clearly defined, you can determine what *types* of career investments you should make. It's your CareerPortfolio investment strategy. It's unique to *you*, a special and unique human being.

➤ Your personal purpose will enable you to clearly assess the costs and benefits of any new career opportunity, and to compare it to other causes and commitments where you could invest your time. You can begin to ask the all-important question: Does this opportunity help me achieve my personal purpose? Always remember: Every moment of your time and focus is precious and could be spent doing *something else*. Your personal purpose will become the benchmark for CareerPortfolio investments.

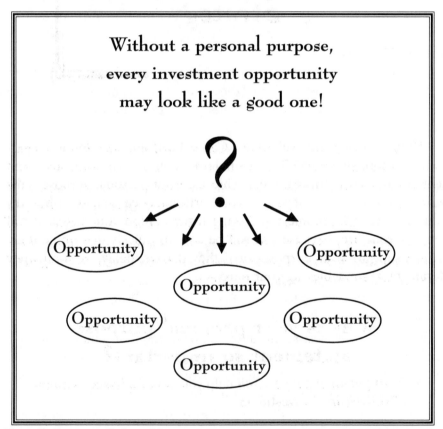

Figure 7: Career confusion without purpose

To begin, don't aim for a perfect definition! Your personal purpose statement does not need to be perfectly defined. It will always be a work in progress. Just putting your thoughts on paper is an excellent start. As time goes on, you can update or completely revise the statement.

Great thinkers of personal purpose

Napoleon Hill was one of the world's greatest modern-day thinkers in the area of personal purpose. Commissioned in 1908 by billionaire steel magnate Andrew Carnegie, Hill spent 40 years of his life researching the success habits of great American leaders of industry.

The common denominator of success, Hill found, is possessing what he called a "definite major purpose." This is a person's overarching grand purpose. But tragically, Hill found that only 2 percent of the world's population consciously developed a definite major purpose. The other 98 percent drifted from one activity to the next, never focused on a bigger life picture.

A computer information systems manager insisted that one of her strengths was being "goal driven." She had set goals and achieved them, one by one. But when asked what her *purpose* in life was, she drew a blank.

The manager became teary-eyed. "Defining my purpose seems like such a monumental decision. I've been putting it off."

Most people think that developing a personal purpose means making a final decision. Underscore this three times: **Developing your personal purpose shouldn't be a daunting task! Your personal purpose will be a work in progress. As your priorities change, so can your purpose. A working draft is a great place to start.** By developing a written working draft, you can begin to refine your ideas over time. You can then determine the right goals and supporting activities that help you develop your CareerPortfolio.

Stephen Covey, best-selling author and business consultant, describes personal purpose as "beginning with the end in mind." He suggests that you visualize your own funeral. Who would be in attendance? What would be said to commemorate your life? Covey underscores the importance of identifying important life priorities and developing action steps for achieving them.

To begin developing your sense of personal purpose, you will need to become a student of your own dreams, skills, and aspirations. Spend a relaxing hour at home or in a quiet place. Complete the lengthy personal journal on the following pages. This will be a good starting point for creating your personal purpose statement.

After you take some time to complete the questions below, it may be helpful for you to select a "purpose pal." You can meet with your purpose pal and discuss your answers and deadlines. The opportunity to gather feedback and establish accountability for your plans can be useful and fun.

Personal Journal...

Developing your personal purpose

You can begin to develop your personal purpose by taking four steps, building on your past successes and considering the present and future.

Step I: Consider your past successes

1. List at least five experiences you've had in recent years where you felt you were making a difference in your world. (For example, perhaps you solved a problem at work, made a difference in others' lives, or did something that helped your neighborhood or community.) Write down at least five examples that come to mind.

    1) _____

    _____

    _____

    2) _____

    _____

    _____

    3) _____

    _____

    _____

4) _____

_____

_____

5) _____

_____

_____

What, exactly, created the opportunity to feel proud of these accomplishments?

_____

_____

_____

Is there a common theme?

_____

_____

_____

Step II: Evaluate your present situation

1. Take one week of your professional life and track how you FEEL about your work.

    What are you doing when you're feeling at your very best, at your prime in your professional life?

_____

_____

_____

What kinds of things excite you?

_____

_____

_____

What kinds of things make you feel content?

_____

_____

_____

In what kind of environment do you find the most contentment:

In a bustling, crowded office?	Yes	No
In a quiet place?	Yes	No
In a room filled with other leaders who are brainstorming solutions?	Yes	No
In a classroom where you are teaching?	Yes	No
Indoors or outdoors?	Yes	No
In a city or a small town?	Yes	No

(Describe the environment as much as possible.)

_____

_____

_____

2. List ideas for how you can contribute your best to:
   Your world in general.

_____

_____

_____

Family.

_____

_____

_____

Work.

_____

_____

_____

Friends.

_____

_____

_____

Community.

_____

_____

_____

3. Make a list of your most important personal values.

_____

_____

_____

_____

_____

_____

4. Now, write down five positive characteristics you like about your-self. For example, diligence to finish a project, creativity, sense of humor, etc.

1) _____

2) _____

3) _____

4) _____

5) _____

Step III: Consider your future

1. How would you like to be remembered many years from now by those who knew you?

_____

_____

_____

2. If you can identify your dreams, chances are, you'll increase your chances of achieving them. What would you do now if there were no risk or chance of failure?

_____

_____

_____

What would fulfilling your dreams look like?

_____

_____

_____

3. What future regrets do you want to avoid?

_____

_____

_____

4. How can you immediately ensure that you can live your purpose every day, without regrets?

_____

_____

_____

Step IV: Writing your personal purpose

Write your personal purpose statement. It can be as long or as short as you desire.

_____

_____

_____

_____

_____

_____

I would like to be remembered 100 years from now as the person who (use answers about your future):

_____

_____

_____

_____

I, _____ , believe that the purpose of my life is to (describe based on your past successes and future dreams):

_____

_____

_____

_____

I will take the following action steps to align my CareerPortfolio with my personal purpose by:

_____

_____

_____

_____

Don't worry if your personal purpose statement isn't perfectly formulated and polished. You have some important ideas that now form a foundation that you can modify as you discover additional insights about yourself and your purpose.

Just as it is for a financial investor, it is *more important to begin even a small* savings program than to wait until you've studied every option, only to discover that the market is constantly changing.

Congratulations! You have drafted your personal purpose statement.

Robyn, the CEO

As president and chief executive officer in a multibillion-dollar Canadian insurance company, Robyn, a CEO, reached a turning point in her career. She sought a major promotion from CEO of a business to officer of the parent company, and was told that she wouldn't be selected due to company politics.

Robyn was qualified for the job. As one who had risen through the financial and operational ranks among the company's 4,000 employees, she had proven herself time and again. But for reasons beyond her control, the CEO's promotion would never happen.

"After years of promotions and corporate life, I was acutely aware that my career didn't measure up to my vision. I had a gnawing sense that something wasn't working. I had limited my own ability by failing to think outside of my corporate environment," Robyn said. "I had spent many years trying to prove myself and please others. I needed to learn how to more fully *be* myself and exploit my talents that were dormant. So I took some time to develop a more defined purpose for my career."

Because of the CareerPortfolio Robyn had built over the years, she was prepared for change (see Figure 9).

- As an economist, she had taught evening college courses and become a respected source of information when Canadian radio and television reporters needed opinions about the economy.

- Preparing courses required constant research on Robyn's part. She was continually growing her knowledge about the field of business and economics.

After much soul searching, Robyn quit her confining corporate job and created a new CareerPortfolio, building from her past successes. Today, Robyn's CareerPortfolio is creative and diverse. Her personal purpose—to unlock the hidden treasures of self-expression and help others expand their own visions—drives her CareerPortfolio investments.

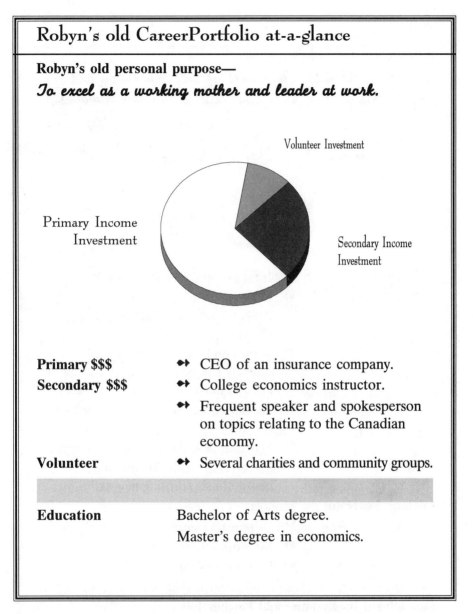

Robyn's old CareerPortfolio at-a-glance

Robyn's old personal purpose—
To excel as a working mother and leader at work.

Volunteer Investment

Primary Income
Investment

Secondary Income
Investment

Primary $$$	↔ CEO of an insurance company.
Secondary $$$	↔ College economics instructor.
	↔ Frequent speaker and spokesperson on topics relating to the Canadian economy.
Volunteer	↔ Several charities and community groups.
Education	Bachelor of Arts degree.
	Master's degree in economics.

Figure 8: Robyn the CEO, before further defining her personal purpose

Robyn's new CareerPortfolio at-a-glance

Robyn's new personal purpose—

To unlock the hidden treasures of self-expression and help others expand their own visions and opportunities.

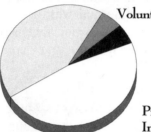

Secondary Income Investment

Volunteer Investment

Lifelong Learning Investment

Primary Income Investment

Primary $$$	❧ International business consultant.
Secondary $$$	❧ Dancer, choreographer, producer of dance shows; performs in Canada and the United States.
	❧ Serves on board of directors of a publicly traded company operating in both Canada and the United States.
	❧ Author, *Quest for Prosperity: The Dance of Success.*
	❧ Workshops and speaking engagements.
Volunteer	❧ Selects charities and community groups, continuously learning new skills.
Lifelong Learning	❧ Voracious reader.
	❧ Writes articles.
	❧ Mentors others.
	❧ Utilizes mentors.

Educational Background and Former Jobs

Bachelor of Arts degree.
Master's degree in economics.
Former college professor, corporate economist, corporate manager, and CEO.

Figure 9: Robyn the CEO, after developing a CareerPortfolio

Robyn started two businesses, a consulting company and a dance production company. Her childhood dream, buried for years under the weight of her corporate responsibilities, sprung forth and came alive as she choreographed and performed in her company's dance theater productions. She later wrote a book about these experiences.

"I discovered how important it is to know your purpose, to understand what you value and what you want based on those values," Robyn told me. "I learned that if people are asleep to their own values, it is easy for them to be controlled by a system."

How did Robyn do it before?

In her early career, Robyn's teaching fit nicely into her CareerPortfolio one night a week. She prepared for classes during lunch hours, occasional evenings, and weekends. Her early years of teaching were the most time consuming because she had to create the foundation course materials. Her experience as an educator set the stage for her recent role as a workshop speaker.

Monday	Tuesday	Wednesday	Thursday	Friday	Saturday	Sunday
		Full-time work 7 a.m. to 5 p.m.			Family time	
Lunch Hour:	Prep for class					
Family time	Evening college teaching	Monthly board meeting 7 p.m.		Family time	Prep for class	

Figure 10: Robyn's former CareerPortfolio schedule as a CEO

How does Robyn do it today?

Today, Robyn splits her week between her consulting business and her theater work. She believes in the benefits of using both the right (creative) and left (analytic) sides of her brain for optimum fulfillment of purpose. Her schedule is shown in Figure 11.

Monday	Tuesday	Wednesday	Thursday	Friday	Saturday	Sunday
Business consulting 7 a.m. to 5 p.m.		Dance Company 7 a.m. to 7 p.m.	Business consulting 7 a. m. to 2 p.m.		Social or family time.	
			Monthly non-profit arts board lunch meeting	Quarterly board meeting (requires travel)		
Social or family time		Dance practice with troups	Social or family time	Troupe or individual dance practice		

Figure 11: Robyn's schedule as CEO of her own company

Payoffs of personal purpose

1. Personal purpose underlies vision and a foundation for change.

When people lose their jobs, they most often use the newspaper and look in the same want-ad section to find the *same kinds* of jobs, even though they don't like what they're currently doing. Your personal purpose can provide a new direction and drive for change. Instead of searching for the same old thing, your purpose will point you in a specific direction that aligns with a planned investment strategy.

2. Personal purpose enables compelling cause and clarity.

Purpose enables you to feel comfortable saying yes and no to career-related investments of time, energy, and effort.

Your life is becoming more cluttered each day. Just think of the information already being exchanged through e-mail. It is estimated that 170 million e-mail users will be sending 5 billion e-mails a day by the year 2005. This equates to roughly 30 e-mails per person per day. When you add phone calls, junk mail, and hundreds of other interruptions into your daily transactions, you see how your life can be filled with distractions that can overshadow meaningful priorities, unless you keep your personal purpose in focus.

3. Personal purpose can provide balance for all parts of your life, not just career-related investments.

Purpose enables you to achieve a balance of earning, learning, and helping others. Purpose guides not only your CareerPortfolio, but also your life portfolio—including your spiritual beliefs and priorities with family and close friends. It provides a focus that is bigger than yourself and your daily challenges. With personal purpose, you can apply a greater amount of wisdom to *all* of the choices and actions of your daily life.

4. Personal purpose is a process of self-discovery.

Your personal purpose is the first step to helping you create a career journey unique to who you are. The journey itself is more important than the final destination. The most important step is to take a step. It will take some time, as you consider your purpose, put your ideas on paper, and refine those thoughts as you gain new insight. Many spend quiet time, or prayer time, where they can contemplate their life direction and consider how to best use the skills and abilities they have.

5. Discovering your purpose doesn't have to be complex.

It will require at least several hours of your thinking time to answer the questions in this chapter. And, it will require that you define the things that are *really* important to you. Then, you can begin making meaningful choices around those priorities.

Consider your time horizon and tolerance for risk

Your life stage (time horizon) and your tolerance for career risk will affect your CareerPortfolio decisions. For example, if you are in your late 60s, you may want to concentrate your time and energy on Volunteer Investments rather than develop a new Secondary Income Investment.

Risk tolerance is the degree of risk you are willing to accept for expanding your career investments beyond your one job. It takes guts and time to begin a business venture, invest in a learning opportunity, or get involved in a volunteer project. Only you can determine your desire to reach beyond your comfort zone.

With your personal purpose, your life stage, and your tolerance for risk in mind, only you can determine your best use of time and what you are willing to give up in order to build a career asset. CareerPortfolios must be tailored to fit our ever-evolving life circumstances. Your CareerPortfolio can help you at any stage of your career life. It's important to recognize that each of us has different abilities for integrating people and projects into our lives. Your capacity to maintain two to four areas of your CareerPortfolio may change over time. See Appendix H for an example of how one might interpret a CareerPortfolio in life stages.

Understanding the general characteristics of life and career changes can enable you to consider the kinds of career investments that are most appropriate, based on your purpose, your available time, and your tolerance for accepting the risk of taking on new career investments. By developing the right investments, you can prepare for an uncertain future. Instead of worrying about turning points that exist in life, your CareerPortfolio investments can help you build new career options that grow exponentially over time.

Overcoming the barriers to personal purpose

1. The Perfectionist Barrier

This is the myth that your personal purpose must be in some perfect form (for example, in some snappy sound bite, refined to 10 words or less). Creating the perfect personal purpose statement then becomes a daunting task.

⇒ **Overcoming the Perfectionist Barrier:** Rather than concentrate on a personal purpose in final form, you should start with a good working draft and continue to tailor it throughout your lifetime.

2. The Cluttered Life Barrier, or, I'm Too Busy

You may truly be challenged by:

➤ Too many social events and not enough quiet time to think.

➤ Reliance on television and being entertained versus participating in your life.

➤ Information overload.

⇒ **Overcoming the Cluttered Life Barrier:** Recognize that the *incidentals* of life will always threaten to overshadow the *important*. Take a weekend and spend it in a quiet way (cancel your appointments for the weekend, if necessary). The point is: STOP! Make an immediate plan to eliminate the business in your daily schedule that does not support your personal purpose. What meetings, television programs, and clutter can you eliminate? What do you get talked into doing that you shouldn't be doing? What career investments can you make to support your personal purpose? After three months, your habits will begin to support your career investment strategy.

3. The Negative Input Barrier from Unsupportive People

All of us have learned how to think from the people with whom we associate. That's why it's vital to spend time with people who are supportive, who have positive, healthy attitudes. Unsupportive people can be an unwelcome source of negative input, even when it involves well-meaning but negative family members, friends, and neighbors.

⇒ **Overcoming the Negative Input Barrier:** You won't be able to eliminate negative or toxic people from your life; however, you can choose to spend more time with those who are supportive of your personal purpose. You can choose to spend less time with those who wear you down and whose behavior is overwhelmingly negative or jealous. Such behavior can rob you of your dignity and sense of purpose.

Instead, integrate into your life positive people and reading materials that bring encouragement and renewed hope. Surround yourself with people who are supportive of your ideas. Don't listen to the naysayers! Get rid of negative television programs and articles that focus on others' gossip and troubles.

Personal Journal...
Identifying and eliminating barriers

List the barriers to personal purpose that affect you the most. (For example, watching too much television or talking on the phone too much.)

1. _____

_____

_____

2. _____

_____

_____

3. _____
_____
_____

4. _____
_____
_____

5. _____
_____
_____

What steps will you take to eliminate those barriers? By when?

1. _____
_____
_____

2. _____
_____
_____

3. _____
_____
_____

4. _____
_____
_____

5. _____
_____
_____

Begin now, start small

Successful financial investors understand that wealth accumulation is a long-term strategy. Successful investors never wait for the perfect mix of investments. They select the choices that make the most sense and begin investing! The investment mix will continually change. The same holds true for investing in your career.

Your CareerPortfolio is not a short-term fix to current-day career risk. You don't have to get it perfect the first time. The most important thing is to know (or begin to understand) your purpose, and to begin aligning your career assets with that purpose. Additional exercises in Appendix C may be useful for further exploration.

Congratulations on developing your personal purpose. You have taken a monumental step in developing the great benchmark upon which all of your career and personal plans can be assessed and put into action. Your personal purpose will serve as the umbrella strategy for career investments discussed throughout this book.

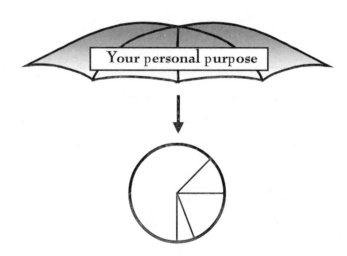

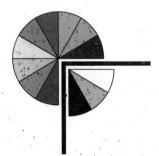

Chapter 4

Your Primary Income Investment: The Value of Purposeful Work

Whether you work for someone else's company or own a business, your Primary Income Investment is a major investment of your time and energy in exchange for income. For most, this is an investment of 40-plus hours a week. For some, it's a flexible or part-time job. For others, it's a commitment to stay home to raise children.

By periodically evaluating your Primary Income Investment, you can ensure this major career asset helps you achieve the ultimate pay-off: your personal purpose.

No matter how you view your Primary Income Investment today, chances are, you'll face the need for a change sometime in the future. There are many triggers that can propel you in a new direction. Sometimes it's a personal crisis that might cause you to reevaluate your life and shift gears. It could be a job loss, the birth of a child, or the death of a loved one.

The benefits of change

Wilma, a deregulated manager, launched a preemptive strike on her Primary Income Investment when she closed out her corporate career. During her 15-year job as a manager for an international phone company, Wilma reached a major life crossroads.

"I was sitting in a business meeting, listening to the talk about how certain things were going to have to change, and suddenly it dawned on me—things *weren't* going to improve...not for a long, long time, possibly never. That's when I realized that I couldn't invest any more of my life hoping and waiting for change. I no longer could see a personal reward for my 60 hours a week. I had relished the divestiture of the telephone industry and embraced competition and the excitement of continual change. But all of a sudden, the work was no longer challenging. It became drudgery."

Sitting in that meeting, Wilma made her decision. Thanks to a CareerPortfolio full of Volunteer and Lifelong Learning Investments, Wilma had many business contacts who were willing to provide jobs, referrals, and supportive advice. She moved out of state and soon began a business as a freelance consultant. She used her corporate skills and also landed a new job as a director of a major university. The hardest part for Wilma was dealing with the emotional part—saying good-bye to a place where she had spent many years.

The benefits of staying put

On the other hand, Gary, an innovator, wants to stay put in his job as a technician in a product manufacturing company. His Primary Income Investment, a 40-hour-a-week line-operations job, provides him with a steady income and benefits while helping him fulfill his purpose, to create innovative technology that improves the lives of others. However, he boosts his career satisfaction with freelance computer and electrical work. This Secondary Income Investment brings additional problem-solving projects into Gary's path. Together, his Primary and Secondary Income Investments are well suited to his career and family goals.

Gary's CareerPortfolio features small but steady Volunteer Investments. He uses his technical skills to provide leadership to his son's Boy Scout troop. Sometimes he volunteers his time fixing elderly neighbors' homes when electrical problems occur. His zest for solving problems and creating solutions is carried forth into each area of his CareerPortfolio, making each investment valuable and meaningful.

Resources for developing a new Primary Income Investment

There are many books about finding a new job and shifting careers. You'll find a number of helpful Web sites listed in the appendices of this book. In addition, you can find a wealth of up-to-date books about getting a job at the public library and at any major bookstore. This chapter focuses on helping you assess your Primary Income Investment to ensure it helps support your personal purpose.

If you work for a large corporation, one of the best available career support resources may be your company's human resources department. Many large corporations offer career fitness and career development services to assist people with making Primary Income Investment decisions. That's because:

➤ More companies today are looking to retain and reposition valuable employees.

➤ Momentum is gaining for companies to candidly recognize that jobs are not a forever commitment.

If you do not have access to career development resources within your company, many community colleges and universities offer career placement and counseling services. You can gain insight on career changing as well as encouragement through such resources. In addition, see Appendix D for a list of online career services.

As you consider your personal purpose and assess the characteristics of your Primary Income Investment, you can become *opportunity*-minded, not job-minded. That is to say, you can proactively look for Primary Income Investment opportunities that help you fulfill your personal purpose.

Personal Journal...

Finding a New Primary Income Investment

Using your personal purpose as a guide, answer the following questions.

1. What new Primary Income Investment options exist in your life?

_____

_____

_____

_____

_____

_____

_____

2. What actions can you immediately take each day to find a better Primary Income Investment, if you currently are not satisfied?

_____

_____

_____

_____

_____

_____

_____

_____

Lisa, the Home-Based Entrepreneur

After trying full-time work, part-time jobs, and telecommuting, Lisa came to terms with the fact that her job conflicted with both her season in life and her personal purpose.

"I needed to be available to my children in a practical and emotional sense while also contributing to the long-term financial security of my family," she said.

Raising four children under the age of 10 produced increasing conflict as she continued to pursue what used to be a rewarding job in a corporate workplace.

"The dependence on nannies to care for my children overpowered any independence I felt as a breadwinner," Lisa said. "That powerful feeling of pay could not balance out the powerless feeling of being absent from home, unaware of the day's moods and motions, unavailable to my children. My quest for more control of my life backfired. I had never felt more vulnerable."

Lisa assessed her ability to provide the same kinds of marketing expertise from home. She discovered she could:

- ➡ Raise her young children while working at home on her own self-directed schedule.
- ➡ Take advantage of technologies (faxes, e-mail, and the Internet) to promote her work and keep in touch with her clients.
- ➡ Focus on a field that constantly is growing (home businesses).
- ➡ Begin her business with a minimal capital outlay.

Before quitting her job and thus her steady source of income, Lisa recruited a few clients who had immediate need of her expertise. Today, she's grown her home-based business to a marketing, communication, and Web site design consultancy that serves small businesses, home businesses, and nonprofit organizations.

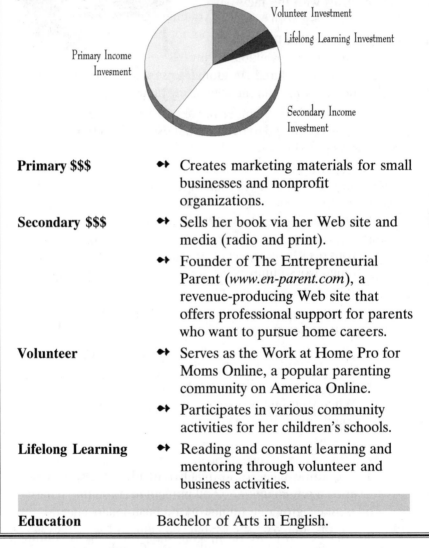

Lisa's CareerPortfolio at-a-glance

Lisa's personal purpose—

To be available to my children in a practical and emotional sense while also contributing to the long-term financial security of my family. Also, to be an advocate for other parents who share the same goals.

Primary $$$	❤ Creates marketing materials for small businesses and nonprofit organizations.
Secondary $$$	❤ Sells her book via her Web site and media (radio and print).
	❤ Founder of The Entrepreneurial Parent (*www.en-parent.com*), a revenue-producing Web site that offers professional support for parents who want to pursue home careers.
Volunteer	❤ Serves as the Work at Home Pro for Moms Online, a popular parenting community on America Online.
	❤ Participates in various community activities for her children's schools.
Lifelong Learning	❤ Reading and constant learning and mentoring through volunteer and business activities.
Education	Bachelor of Arts in English.

Figure 12: Lisa the Home-Based Entrepreneur

Lisa is also the author of *How to Raise a Family and a Career Under One Roof: A Parent's Guide to Home Business* and is the founder of The Entrepreneurial Parent (*www.en-parent.com*). The Entrepreneurial Parent is a partnership with fellow work-at-home moms. It's a growing work/family resource for home-based entrepreneurs and career professionals who are looking for alternative work options.

As she pursues her home career, Lisa advises other parents how to start home-based businesses, a volunteer activity that benefits others while serving as a marketing tool for her book and Web site.

Lisa's tips for home-based business success:

➤➤ View your work and family life as an integrated whole, rather than keeping them detached in separate compartments of your life. Do this on a day-by-day basis as well as on a one-, five-, and 10-year plan. This will help you recognize that your work life will ebb and flow according to your family life, and that it's okay to spend a disproportionate amount of time on each at various seasons of your life.

➤➤ Post your personal purpose, or inspirational quotes that reflect your personal purpose, in a prominent spot on your desk. This can help you stay focused on your long-range work/family goals and is an effective tool to use when you must prioritize your workload.

➤➤ Whether you work for yourself or someone else, pick your projects carefully. Go after projects that will enhance your career, resume, and/or work portfolio, not just the most impressive job title or client account.

➤➤ Your marketability depends on tangible end results. When your family is young, the quality of your projects counts more than the quantity. In other words, do less and do it *well.*

➤➤ Develop your niche through a variety of skills and activities. For instance, supplement your core job responsibility by teaching, writing, speaking, and/or consulting, either within a corporate framework or as an independent.

Lisa places a priority on making time for focused volunteer projects that help to build her business *and* her CareerPortfolio.

How does Lisa do it?

Monday	Tuesday	Wednesday	Thursday	Friday	Saturday	Sunday
Marketing/Web site consulting 8 a.m. to noon				Chores and errands 8 a.m. to 5 p.m.	Family time	
Noon to 5 p.m. with children						
Family time						
After kids are asleep, occasional night projects, including volunteer investments.						

Figure 13: Lisa's schedule

Signs of alignment with your purpose

How can you be sure that your Primary Income Investment is purposeful? Here are several clues.

➤ Your Primary Income Investment directly supports your personal purpose.

➤ Your Primary Income Investment indirectly supports your ability to achieve your personal purpose through other venues. For example, it provides the financial stability to help you launch your Secondary Income Source, which may be more purposeful.

➤ You're excited about going to work each day.

➤ You're recognized for your contributions.

➤ You're growing in your knowledge and expertise.

➤ You have future plans with respect to your Primary Income Investment.

Personal Journal...
Signs of synergy with personal purpose

Evaluate your Primary Income Investment. If you can answer yes to most of the following questions, your Primary Income Investment may be a good match with your personal purpose.

1. Does your Primary Income Investment match your personal purpose?   Yes   No

    If yes, how? _____

    _____

    _____

    _____

    _____

    _____

2. Whether you work inside your home or in the workplace, are you optimistic about the new day at hand?   Yes   No

    Are you glad to be there?   Yes   No

3. Are you viewed by your peers, superiors, and subordinates as being credible and competent?   Yes   No

4. Do you have the right aptitude and skills for your Primary Income Investment today?   Yes   No

5. Do you know what your company's future needs are?

                            Yes   No

    Do you find ways to grow your knowledge with respect to those future needs?   Yes   No

    If yes, how? _____

    _____

    _____

    _____

    _____

6. Do you know why your contribution is vital to your company?

    Yes   No

7. Do you see the job at hand as a step in a continuum or career journey—not as the end of the journey?   Yes   No

8. Do you know the trade-offs of selecting your current Primary Income Investment versus other opportunities? (List the trade-offs here.)   Yes   No

    _____

    _____

    _____

    _____

    _____

9. Are you able to integrate life moments with work moments and bridge the gap between work and family life?   Yes   No

    If so, what in your current job permits you to do this?

    _____

    _____

    _____

    _____

    _____

10. Do you have a career safety net in case you lose your Primary Income Investment?   Yes   No

Signs of change on the horizon

Perhaps you are in the midst of a Primary Income Investment transition. You may sense that a change is in the works, yet for now, you lack the desire or courage to make a change. The following signs may serve as a warning when change is needed:

> What used to bring you a sense of reward (the challenge, the positive feedback, etc.) doesn't feel good anymore.

> You discover that you cannot live your personal values in your workplace. For example, you are asked to do things, say things, or write things that aren't compatible with your values.

> You doubt that you're making a difference.

> The work is no longer challenging.

> You begin to take notice of things that didn't used to bother you. You begin keeping score on people, events, and circumstances that upset you.

Personal Journal...
Steps for evaluating a change or transition

Candidly answer the following questions:

1. Describe your relationships within your current job or Primary Income Investment.

_____

_____

_____

_____

_____

2. What actions can you *immediately* take to cultivate closer or more effective working relationships with your employer and/or colleagues at work?

_____

_____

_____

_____

3. What will be your next step if the above actions do not make a significant difference in the way you're feeling about your current Primary Income Investment?

_____

_____

_____

4. Set a deadline for observing significant improvement in how you view your Primary Income Investment as it relates to helping you achieve your personal purpose.

Deadline: _____

Signs of conflict with personal purpose

Your Primary Income Investment is blocking you from fulfilling your personal purpose if:

> ➤ You feel trapped by your Primary Income Investment.

> ➤ You're worn and weathered by office politics and responsibilities, and have little or no desire to fix or address the problems.

> ➤ You skip work.

> ➤ You feel guilty because there's the constant sense of compromising your life and life values.

> ➤ You feel burned out and depressed, and your body language and facial expressions show it.

> ➤ You internalize your dissatisfaction and it begins to take on external symptoms, such as illness, bouts of crying, and so on.

Personal Journal...

Assessing your Primary Income Investment

This Personal Journal exercise will help you assess whether your Primary Income Investment currently is a valuable career asset in your CareerPortfolio.

1. List your personal purpose draft from the previous chapter.

   _____

   _____

   _____

   _____

   _____

2. Does your current Primary Income Investment help you achieve your purpose (either directly or indirectly)?   Yes   No

   If yes, describe how:

   _____

   _____

   _____

   If no, describe why:

   _____

   _____

   _____

3. Is there a good reason your Primary Income Investment does not directly support your purpose?   Yes   No

   Describe.

   _____

   _____

   _____

4. Is it time to make a change?   Yes   No

5. By when will you have a new Primary Income Investment?

_____

6. What steps or action do you plan to take?

_____

_____

_____

7. By when? _____

Primary Income Investment
in summary

➤ Know your purpose.

➤ Recognize the signs of synergy, transition, and total dissatisfaction.

➤ Develop a network of supportive colleagues who can help you overcome self-doubt and provide encouraging advice.

➤ Finally, get comfortable with being uncomfortable! Change is never easy.

Congratulations for assessing your Primary Income Investment. In Chapter 5, you'll discover the benefits of building a Secondary Income Investment into your CareerPortfolio.

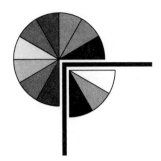

Chapter 5

Your Secondary Income Investment: The Value of Plan B

Think about your Primary Income Investment. What would happen if you suddenly lost it? Or, what would you do if you realized that it conflicts with your personal purpose? Would you have other meaningful options for meeting your financial needs?

Here's an even tougher question if you are employed: Are you willing to work for yourself as hard as you're willing to work for someone else?

A Secondary Income Investment can be an effective way to add learning and new options to your CareerPortfolio. Although owning and operating a business may not be for everyone, many are discovering that having a Plan B creates flexibility and protection against being downsized, merged, and bankrupted into unemployment. Moreover, a Secondary Income Investment can be integrated into existing career investments as time permits. It can be:

➤ A financial investment.

➤ A consulting project performed once a year or more or an income-producing project you choose to conduct once a year. For example, you could write or provide analysis for a special report or conduct an income-tax business during tax season, taking on a few clients.

➤ Any number of products or services sold to paying clients.

➤ A weekly or daily business you conduct, such as custom calligraphy on business cards.

➤ A seasonal business (holidays, summer, etc.).

Your Secondary Income Investment is *not* the same as moonlighting. Moonlighting is a term that implies a second job working for someone else. A Secondary Income Investment is something that *you own and manage*. With a Secondary Income Investment, *you* are the boss. And, chances are, if your Secondary Income Investment is successful, it could become your Primary Income Investment someday!

Even those who own their own businesses can benefit from diversifying by adding new product lines or types of customers. It's estimated that more than 16 percent of the American workforce are free agents who work for themselves. These are people who move from project to project and who work on their own, sometimes for months at a time, sometimes for days.

Even free agents are questioning the wisdom of investing all their human capital in a single employer. Not only is it more interesting to have six clients instead of one boss, it also may be safer.

The payoff:
Entrepreneurial skills in demand

Today, more companies are seeking employees who "act like they own the business." With a Secondary Income Investment, you can develop entrepreneurial skills that most companies are aggressively seeking to compete in a fast-changing, global economy. Your new experiences will help you build confidence and options for new opportunities. (See Figures 14 and 15.)

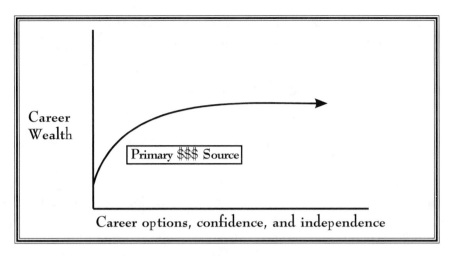

Figure 14: Options with Primary Income Investment only

The tables of influence on this page depict how a professional might view his or her career wealth. If you focus all of your time and energy on one job, especially if you work for someone else, you may reduce your opportunity to build career wealth over time. At first, your knowledge wealth is driven upward. At some point, however, you may find that your learning opportunities reach a plateau.

Your Secondary Income Investment, on the other hand, can provide you with additional learning opportunities not otherwise possible.

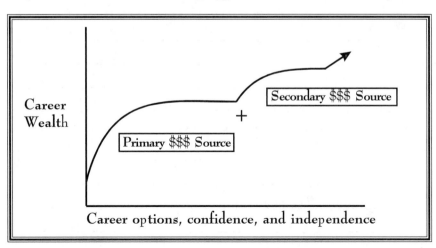

Figure 15: Options with Primary and Secondary Income Investments combined

By developing a Secondary Income Investment, you can:

➤ Gain new entrepreneurial skills.

➤ Ensure that your existing skills do not become obsolete.

➤ Gain fresh confidence in your abilities.

➤ Gain income beyond your current Primary Income Investment.

➤ Position yourself for a new career direction.

Your Secondary Income Investment can give you the extra confidence of *having options*. Once you begin to understand your personal purpose, you can continually ask yourself, "What are other options for my skills, desires, and abilities? How can my background fill an unmet need?"

―――――⊗―――――

Personal Journal...
Defining the product or service

Answer the following questions:

1. What product or service could you offer that someone else might be willing to buy?

_____

_____

_____

_____

2. Describe more about the product or service here. Why would your product or service be in demand?

_____

_____

_____

_____

3. How would your product or service be better than those offered by competitors?

   _____

   _____

   _____

   _____

4. What, generally, would your customers be willing to pay for this product or service?

   _____

   _____

5. Where would you conduct the business if you were to offer the product or service?

   _____

   _____

The beauty of Plan B

To protect yourself from career risk, you always should know the answers to "what if" questions. What if you lost your job and had to find work somewhere else? What if you had a financial catastrophe? What if you could start your own business?

Instead of feeling trapped or victimized by your job or Primary Income Investment, you can think more positively when you see new options on the horizon. You will always know, no matter what happens, that you have something valuable to supply—something that customers demand.

But sadly, many people don't realize they *have* options when it comes to their careers. With anything in life, once you know your options, you have the power to negotiate a solution. The best advice for protecting yourself against career risk is: Always know your options!

Negotiating experts equate having options to having a "Best Alternative to the Negotiated Agreement." If you haven't thought carefully about what you will do if things don't go your way, you may be:

➤ Too optimistic, assuming you have many other job options and career moves.

➤ Too pessimistic.

The only way to know for sure, when you're negotiating any outcome in life, is to explore and plan your options. Your CareerPortfolio is a tool for helping you do this.

Lexi, the Organizer

Lexi, a 24-year-old home-space designer, works for a national closet company. An architect by background, Lexi discovered an overwhelming demand for better household organization. Her clients desperately needed ideas that went beyond the retail closet store's scope.

"People would describe their home clutter to me. I struggled with the thought of people leaving the store with no practical help with what they said they needed—ideas for getting organized at home. I visualized their mess! I saw an opportunity to develop a business that would use my design background, allow for easy and flexible hours, and provide a rewarding way to help others," Lexi said.

While working full time at the closet company, Lexi fell into a simple and lucrative Secondary Income Investment. What would seem fortuitous was actually Lexi's perception of a real, market-based customer need—an overwhelming number of people who needed to get organized.

"My purpose is to help others live peaceful, enjoyable lives," she said. "I do this by helping people use their home space more efficiently. I tour the home and point out things they can do to be better organized. There's no inventory or financial investment involved. Best yet, there's no follow-up work once I leave the place."

Lexi's CareerPortfolio at-a-glance

Lexi's personal purpose—
To be the best wife and mother I can be, and to serve others through sharing my skills and resources.

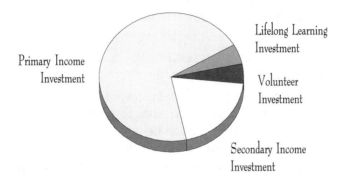

Primary $$$	➤➤ Design consultant for a major closet company.
Secondary $$$	➤➤ Personal consultant in home organizing.
Volunteer	➤➤ Serves as a big sister with local Big Brothers, Big Sisters program.
	➤➤ Writes HotFlash bulletin for a professional woman's newsletter.
Lifelong Learning	➤➤ Takes seminars and design-related courses every few months.
Education	Bachelor of Science degree in Interior Design.

Figure 16: Lexi the Organizer

After work and sometimes during lunch hours, Lexi visits clients' homes and provides on-the-spot, practical ideas for getting organized.

Figure 16 shows Lexi's CareerPortfolio. Her Secondary Income Investment provides the following payoffs:

- ➤ At the end of her visit, she charges an hourly fee.
- ➤ No follow-up responsibilities are required unless the client chooses to hire Lexi to help sort household items (which is rare).
- ➤ Lexi doesn't need to spend money on advertising; all of her business is gained by referrals.
- ➤ Her consulting business can provide a new career direction if Lexi chooses to work fewer hours. Eventually, she says, she wants to be a stay-at-home mother once she and her husband have children. Her Secondary Income Investment could become a flexible Primary Income Investment.

How does Lexi do it?

Monday	Tuesday	Wednesday	Thursday	Friday	Saturday	Sunday
	Full-time work 8 a.m. to 5 p.m. at closet design store.				One or two clients before noon	Family time
Lunch hour: Visit clients for Secondary Income Investment						
Volunteer activity once every two weeks					Family time	
Two-hour block for Secondary Income Investment	Social/ family time	Volunteer activity	Two-hour block for Secondary Income Investment	Social/ family time		

Figure 17: Lexi's schedule

- Lexi's consulting business benefits her Primary Income Investment and her role as a closet designer, because new business occasionally is drawn into the retail store. Likewise, she often finds clients through her Primary Income Investment.

- Lexi writes articles for a women's business organization, featuring tips for being better organized at home and in the office, as a volunteer. This, in turn, generates more Primary and Secondary business.

- Lexi's projects require no working capital, no employees, and no time beyond what she chooses to schedule. What more could she ask for?

Getting started

Granted, not everyone is destined to own a business or embark on freelance projects. With enthusiasm, however, you can build a successful Secondary Income Investment if you provide a product or service that others are willing to buy. See Appendix E for more information about launching your Secondary Income Investment.

If you own a business already, you may want to consider diversifying your business with a second product line or division. Having a Secondary Income Investment within your business can provide additional revenue and can help you hedge risk.

The best types of Secondary Income Investments are those that allow you to earn, learn, and grow as you go. You should make this investment as achievable and practical as possible. Here are a few guidelines to help you get started:

> Find work that is important or interesting.

> Be sure the work supports your personal purpose. For example, Lexi enjoys encouraging others to live peaceful lives. Her home-organizing business supports her purpose and conveniently fits within her schedule.

➤ Strive to become excellent at the work or project you select. Capitalize on your personal strengths.

➤ Assess the marketability of the work, doing homework about the potential business. Focus on understanding why the business exists.

➤ Be sure the work fits into your schedule and lifestyle and that your life priorities are not threatened. Your business will require investments of time and financial resources.

➤ Implement action steps to achieve profit for the business.

➤ Don't start a business that requires your spouse or life's savings to support you. Remember, you are in a testing phase. Start modestly. Less is more. It may take years to recover your initial investment if you are not serious about sticking with it.

➤ Once you know that your Secondary Income Investment is going to be a success, then you can decide to commit more financial resources.

➤ Don't quit your Primary Income Investment during your Secondary Income Investment startup.

➤ If a Secondary Income Investment is not right for you at this time, you can gather ideas and consider developing this CareerPortfolio asset in the future.

Finding the time

Starting a business does not require superhuman talents. Two qualities are required: the willingness to act to overcome all obstacles, and the overpowering desire to change your life from what it is to what you want it to be.

How can you find time to pursue a Secondary Income Investment when you're already busy? By answering the following questions, you may find a few practical ways to fit a Secondary Income Investment into your busy schedule.

➤ Given your circumstances, could you find one evening per week? A few hours a day? A weekend per year? It's been said that if you can research or practice something one hour a day, six days a week, you can become an expert at it!

➤ Can you use your lunch hour in a more productive way to conduct your Secondary Income Investment?

➤ Is there an annual project that someone needs, to give you the experience of being a consultant?

➤ Are there projects you could complete on a seasonal basis (such as tax preparation during tax time)?

➤ Could you watch less TV?

Your Secondary Income Investment can be as fun, flexible, and achievable as your imagination allows. It should not be an overwhelming experience that monopolizes your life and stresses you out.

To begin considering your Secondary Income Investment, complete the exercises in the Personal Journal on the next page.

TV: The time waster

⇒ The average American watches an equivalent of 52 days of TV a year.

⇒ By age 65, the average adult will have spent nine years of his or her life watching TV.

⇒ Each week, the average child between ages 2 and 11 watches 1,200 minutes of TV, yet only spends 39 minutes talking with his or her parents.

⇒ Each year, the average teen spends 900 hours in school and 1,500 hours watching TV. This sets the pattern for watching TV in adulthood versus accomplishing other goals and projects.

Source: TV-Free America, 1999.

Personal Journal...

Brainstorming your business start-up

1. List your personal purpose in the "umbrella" diagram below. Fill in your desired Secondary Income Investment underneath the purpose umbrella. Describe how it aligns with your purpose.

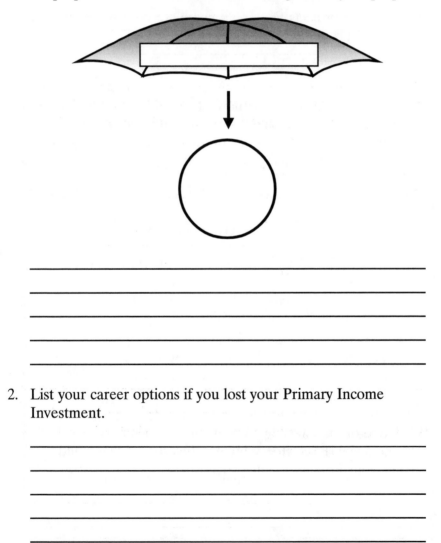

_____

_____

_____

_____

_____

2. List your career options if you lost your Primary Income Investment.

_____

_____

_____

_____

3. If you could pursue something different from your Primary Income Investment, what would that be?

_____

_____

_____

_____

What appeals to you?

_____

_____

_____

_____

4. What have you always wanted to do that you have not pursued?

_____

_____

_____

_____

What hobbies or special skills might you deploy to develop a secondary source of income?

_____

_____

_____

_____

5. What kind of time would you be willing to spend each week to cultivate a viable Secondary Income Investment that could become your Primary Income Investment?

_____

_____

6. Are there people in your life with whom you'd consider partnering from time to time, to create additional momentum and synergy?

List potential business partner/associate	What kind of benefit or synergy exists?

7. List additional insights you received by completing the answers above.

Ideas for your Secondary Income Investment

Your career wealth is no longer dependent on a location. Thanks to technology, your Secondary Income Investment can be wherever you are—at home or during travel. This can enable you to develop an enjoyable, convenient Secondary Income Investment without significant major expenses, such as an office or employees.

The top 10 home-based businesses are:

1. Business consulting and services.

2. Computer programming and services.

3. Financial consulting and services.

4. Marketing and advertising.

5. Medical practice and services.

6. Graphics and visual arts.

7. Public relations and publicity.

8. Real estate.

9. Writing.

10. Independent sales.

Source: Link Resources Corporation, New York, NY, 1997.

More ideas: Putting hobbies to work

Some people gravitate toward their Secondary Income Investment by exploiting things that they enjoy doing. Here are some hobbies that could pay off as Secondary Income Investments.

Your skill	Potential business
Playing an instrument	Teaching, music lessons
Being good at a sport	Teaching private sports lessons—golf, swimming, athletic training
Writing	Writing guest columns, movie reviews, and perspective articles for publications
Speaking in front of audiences	Organizational training or facilitating
Reading	Providing high-level summaries for businesses, publications, and educators for leading-edge research
Research and learning	Providing research assistance
Travel	Providing tour services; writing travel reviews

Companies benefit from entrepreneurial employees

Employees who have Secondary Income Investments most often are entrepreneurial professionals who are forward thinking.

If you are an employer, realize that your employees who own businesses are gaining valuable information and skills that can benefit your company. You can take an active role in encouraging employees to build new skills through a Secondary Income Investment. In doing so, you can be a leader in developing confident, flexible employees who add even more value to your business.

Micropreneuring in the new millennium

When most people think of entrepreneurs, they think of risk takers who borrow to the hilt, hire employees, and open up an expensive storefront, risking their personal savings for a business that could go belly-up.

That's not Michael the Millionaire Micropreneur's idea of the perfect business. Michael was teaching organizational behavior and management classes as a college professor when a colleague suggested he spend his sabbatical turning his time-management seminar into a book.

While Michael continued teaching, he birthed a new career as an author (new Primary Income Investment) and guest lecturer (Secondary Income Investment). His first book paved the way for three more books. "I never hired anybody, I never borrowed any money, I didn't quit my day job until I was well on my way. I was not a big risk taker, and I'm not a workaholic," he said in a July 22, 1998 article in *The Arizona Republic*.

One of Michael's books became his big money-maker and launching pad for a full-time writing and speaking career. Today, he advises people to select something related to what they succeeded at in the job world. "Loving what you do is half the battle," he counsels. "Marketability is the other half. It's not what you know, it's what sells, and how well it sells, that determines how successful your business is."

Virtues of the entrepreneur

Characteristics of the successful entrepreneur build and evolve over time. How many of these describe you?

⇒ Self-confident.

⇒ Aggressive.

⇒ Meticulous.

⇒ Self-disciplined.

⇒ Intelligent.

⇒ Determined.

⇒ Inventive.

⇒ Capable.

⇒ Experienced.

⇒ Careful but willing to take calculated risks.

⇒ Inspiring to others.

⇒ Charming and personable yet capable of being ruthless when necessary.

⇒ Honest with self and others.

⇒ Has clear personal goals.

⇒ Has a good sense of humor.

⇒ Has a successful track record and strong financial backing.

From your home to the world

With technology on your side, owning your own business has never been easier. As the United States Small Business Administration points out, a quiet revolution has moved the American economy from the industrial age to the information age.

According to the SBA, we're experiencing the most rapid shift the world has ever known, moving from a society of corporate giants to sole proprietors at a rate of 2 percent per year since the mid-1990s. Why such a wellspring of small businesses? Many who were downsized during the 1980s and 1990s started their own sole proprietorship companies.

About 65 percent of America's fast-track firms, both large and small, use outsourced firms to complete numerous tasks, according to a survey by Coopers and Lybrand. Fast-track firms are companies that want to work only in their core competencies. That way, they keep costs down and can focus exclusively on the areas where they have a competitive advantage. Because outsourcing (hiring temporary workers who are paid by the hour or project) allows firms to focus on areas of core business, reduce debt, and grow profit margins, it can be good news for those of us who can fill these niches. This brings many opportunities for people just like you!

With Internet technology at your fingertips, new forms of Secondary Income Investments are possible today. Virtual retailing is one example. Book distributors such as Amazon.com and BarnesandNoble.com invite digital entrepreneurs to earn commissions on referrals from their home pages. It's getting easier to become an effortless digital retailer. All you need is a home page. You'll never need to touch the goods, or manage order flow, or take a payment.

Personal Journal...

Finding time to integrate a Secondary Income Investment

1. For the next year of your life, what days of the week are best for integrating your Secondary Income Investment?

_____

_____

What hours are best?

_____

2. Consider which of your activities do not match your personal purpose and could be removed from your schedule. List them below.

_____

_____

_____

_____

_____

3. Now list other miscellaneous activities that get in the way of developing a Secondary Income Investment.

_____

_____

_____

_____

4. Write a specific plan to reduce or remove non-value-added activities.

Activities to reduce/remove	By this date:	Helps you free up this time:
_____	_____	_____
_____	_____	_____
_____	_____	_____
_____	_____	_____
_____	_____	_____
_____	_____	_____
_____	_____	_____
_____	_____	_____

Secondary Income
Investment in summary

➤ Know your personal purpose.

➤ Answer the questions in this chapter. Explore how a Secondary Income Investment might help you fulfill your purpose in a rich and rewarding way.

➤ Take the appropriate steps and tap into people who can provide advice.

➤ If a Secondary Income Investment is not feasible for you right now, at least you've gained helpful ideas for future endeavors.

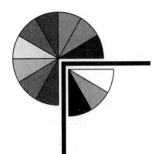

Chapter 6

Your Volunteer Investments: The Value of Serving Others

Purposeful volunteerism can be one of the most rewarding tools in your CareerPortfolio. When you contribute your time and talents to help a worthwhile cause, you can gain the rewards of service while growing your career wealth.

If you are not ready to embark on a Secondary Income Investment, a volunteer opportunity could be a powerful strategy to help you build career wealth. Whether you volunteer at the grassroots level for causes in which you believe, or serve on a board of directors, your Volunteer Investment can bring a tremendous sense of personal and professional reward.

Types of volunteerism

Volunteerism tends to fall into five major categories. Consider the following areas, and then ask yourself what your passion is.

Human services: Such as volunteering to help the homeless, the aging, people with special needs, victims of domestic violence or child abuse, and so forth.

Arts and culture: Such as volunteering to support a museum, theater, and or place where culture and art are promoted.

Education: Such as volunteering at your child's school, serving on a parent committee or school board, teaching a workshop in your community without being paid, or teaching a class at your church, synagogue, or place of worship.

Civic: Such as getting involved with your local chamber of commerce or volunteering for sports activities or special events that are focused on improving the economic well-being of the community.

Environment: Such as volunteering for a group that focuses on the preservation of land, water, and air quality.

Here's what volunteer investments can do for your future.

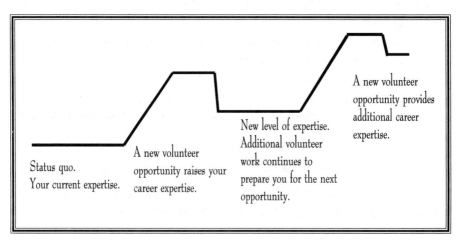

Figure 18: Volunteer Investments can boost your career wealth

Volunteer Investment payoffs

➤ Volunteerism can enable you to reach the end of your life knowing that you used your talent in a way that impacted other lives for the better. For example, a dentist in California donates one day per month to treat poor children whose families cannot afford dental care. Someday, he will look back on his career with great satisfaction, without regrets of having served only himself.

➤ Volunteer Investments give you the opportunity to be an owner, versus a renter, in your community. This means that you have chosen to contribute to society, rather than sit back and complain about the problems.

➤ Volunteerism provides the chance to cultivate relationships and associations with other professionals of influence and leadership abilities. This includes new potential business contacts and customers that can benefit your business.

➤ You can gain leadership skills, including planning, project management, and motivational abilities.

➤ You can quickly find no-risk and/or low-risk exposure to new career experiences and responsibilities.

➤ You may be able to manage or oversee a budget (or a larger budget than your current work situation), which is excellent experience.

➤ You can work in a team environment for a cause that team members are passionate to see succeed.

➤ If you are a stay-at-home parent, volunteering can add career experiences to your CareerPortfolio without the pressure of having to work for pay.

Jim, the City Councilman

Jim, a corporate risk management (insurance) analyst, discovered that he wanted to make a difference in the quality of life in his community. Having a child with special health needs, he turned his focus toward children's issues and became involved with a local children's cancer center.

As he volunteered, Jim found great personal reward in learning about his community's needs. Having had his confidence built up by this initial community service, he then decided to run for city council and was elected. In this new role, Jim climbed a steep learning curve and developed new skills that greatly increased his career wealth.

"The biggest career enhancement so far is my ability to make decisions, take a position, and be accountable to stand behind the decision," Jim said. "In my job, I made recommendations to others who made the final decision. As a city councilman, I have to know the issues and make decisions that impact thousands of lives, such as gun control and building new freeways. I've developed my ability to listen to others and balance work, volunteerism, and family. I've grown as a leader and decision maker, both on and off the job."

On the job, Jim sets short-term goals to keep focused on his work priorities while accomplishing his Volunteer Investment on his own time. He often returns civic-related phone calls during his lunch hour, a practice supported by his employer.

Jim doesn't have time for a Secondary Income Investment, and his Lifelong Learning Investment is accomplished through his volunteer role (he reads a number of documents and newspapers daily to keep up on the local issues; see Figure 19).

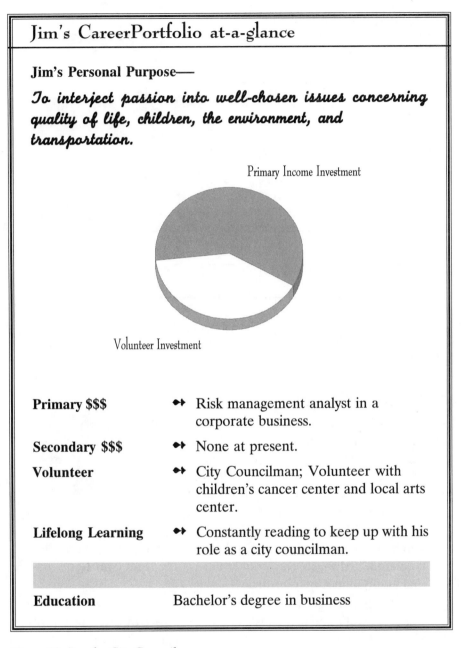

Jim's CareerPortfolio at-a-glance

Jim's Personal Purpose—

To interject passion into well-chosen issues concerning quality of life, children, the environment, and transportation.

Primary Income Investment

Volunteer Investment

Primary $$$	➤ Risk management analyst in a corporate business.
Secondary $$$	➤ None at present.
Volunteer	➤ City Councilman; Volunteer with children's cancer center and local arts center.
Lifelong Learning	➤ Constantly reading to keep up with his role as a city councilman.
Education	Bachelor's degree in business

Figure 19: Jim the City Councilman

How does Jim do it?

Monday	Tuesday	Wednesday	Thursday	Friday	Saturday	Sunday
		Full-time work 8 a.m. to 5 p.m.				
		Risk management analyst			Family time	
Lunch hour: Return phone calls as needed.						
Family time		City council meetings	Family time			
Evening reading after kids are asleep.		6 to 11 p.m.	Evening reading			

Figure 20: Jim's schedule

Al, the PR Man

Nearly a half-century ago, Al founded a public relations firm in Chicago. By developing numerous Volunteer Investments as part of his business and personal CareerPortfolio, Al, still the company's CEO, is a role model for entrepreneurship, leadership, and philanthropy.

"In 1957, I made a cold phone call to a guy named Ray Kroc who had a handful of old red and white drive-ins around the Chicago area," Al said. "Ray asked me to come right over to discuss his 15-cent hamburger business."

Al felt strongly that the McDonald's restaurants could be uniquely positioned in the fast-food marketplace by offering a spirit of philanthropy. "We believe that if you want to be different, you ought to prove that you're different by getting involved with the community. People want to patronize places they like and trust," Al said.

Al's CareerPortfolio at-a-glance

Al's Personal Purpose for his business—

To make a profit and contribute back to the community where we serve.

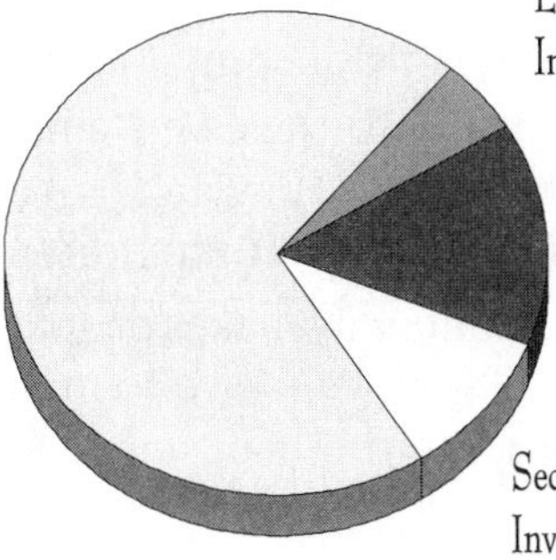

Lifelong Learning Investment

Volunteer Investment

Primary Income Investment

Secondary Income Investment

Primary $$$	➤	Public relations business, advertising
Secondary $$$	➤	Other business pursuits related to the communication profession
Volunteer	➤	Al allows employees to serve on nonprofit boards and for volunteer investments.
	➤	His business gives cash support to specific charitable causes.
Lifelong Learning	➤	Al's business offers workshops and learning opportunities for employees, promoting lifelong learning.
Education		Bachelor of Science in commerce

Figure 21: Al the PR Man

Al's public relations and advertising firm helped McDonald's develop the concept of Ronald McDonald, a friendly clown who reached out to children. For the past 40 years, as McDonald's went from being an unknown burger joint to a household word in the United States and in 100 other countries, Al helped develop cause-related marketing and public-relations strategies that put a friendly face behind the company's hamburgers.

In his own business Al encourages his employees to develop a heart for serving others by encouraging them to get involved in their communities. He encourages his employees to take time to volunteer during the business day and considers this to be part of his corporate investment in the community.

"Giving to your community makes people feel good about where they work," Al said. "Sure, you have to make profits—that's your first obligation in order to stay in business. However, I like to think that my employees are happy working here because we do encourage them to get involved."

How does Al do it?

Monday	Tuesday	Wednesday	Thursday	Friday	Saturday	Sunday
	Full-time work 9 a.m. to 6 p.m. Run the business. Meet with clients. Community meetings relevant to the business.				Relaxation, reading, hobbies, and down time.	
	Evening: Volunteer board meetings and civic/social events.					

Figure 22: Al's schedule

Getting your foot in the door

Integrating volunteerism into your life will require you to step outside your comfort zone. For example, you will need to take the time to volunteer. You may be thrust together with people with whom you might not have much in common, at least at first. You may be used to being in control of outcomes at your workplace. In your volunteer situation, however, you may not be able to control all of the outcomes, nor know all the answers to the challenges that you're addressing. This is all part of the learning experience.

At times, you may be stretched way out of your comfort zone. This can result in a tremendous amount of professional growth. And there are additional benefits; volunteers usually are supported by experienced help from the organization's staff and other volunteers. You may not see this kind of collaboration in the traditional corporate environment.

"You'd be surprised at the amount of responsibility you can assume as a volunteer," said Mike Heron, a national vice president for the American Cancer Society. "There's not one nonprofit entity that would not accept your help, if you are sufficiently prepared to know a little about what you'd like to accomplish. You can run big programs, from inception to implementation, with a soft place to land in case you make a few mistakes. You can quickly gain responsibility in taking on jobs completely outside of your current responsibilities."

By giving of ourselves and reaching outward to the world in which we live, we receive not only personal growth, but fulfillment. By sowing, we can reap not only personal satisfaction, but a greater sense of meaning, which allows us to lead fuller, richer lives.

Volunteering with purpose

There are fundamental ingredients for obtaining good volunteers. Here is the "R formula" used by volunteer placement professionals, as shared with me by Lucia Causey, community philanthropist and former director of The Volunteer Center of Phoenix:

➤ Recruit the volunteer.

➤ Refer the volunteer to the agency.

➤ Recognize the volunteer.

➤ Retain the volunteer.

➤ Reflect upon your lessons learned.

➤ Research to improve the program.

➤ Reward the volunteer.

Agencies are hungry for dedicated volunteers. Ideally, in a win-win situation, both the volunteer and the agency should have a process for recruiting and retaining volunteers. (A list of volunteer recruitment agencies is listed in Appendix F for your reference.)

When you explore a volunteer pursuit, recognize that your special talents and skills will be highly appreciated by the right entity. Know your purpose for wanting to volunteer. Do not be intimidated by interviews or questions about your skills.

Assessing Volunteer Investments

When assessing the Volunteer Investments, I recommend five criteria for you to consider with respect to your personal purpose:

1. The cause.

2. The experience, or expertise, gained.

3. The network.

4. Your ability to contribute.

5. Your available time.

1. The cause

Does the cause match your personal purpose? Will this experience help you fulfill your personal purpose and bring joy to others? How does the opportunity support and mesh with your personal purpose?

⇒ **Tip:** Once you've discovered your personal purpose, make a study of causes that align with your purpose. Talk to friends about their volunteer experiences. You'll quickly recognize when volunteer opportunities are a good match.

2. The experience, or expertise, gained

Will giving to others add one or more valuable experiences or areas of expertise beyond what your current job or business pursuits offer? It's okay to look for, and expect to gain, needed experience outside of your current job.

⇒ **Tip:** Set clear, realistic goals for gaining the desired volunteer experience. Although you want to help others, you also want to develop specific skills, explore certain careers, and make contacts that can help you in your new pursuits.

⇒ **Tip:** Interview for your volunteer position as if it is a paid position. Request a job description. Attend training opportunities recommended by the agency. Ask for a periodic review of your work. Develop records of your performance.

⇒ **Tip:** If you are looking to make a drastic career change, or if you are a college student wanting to build your experience, you can contact a nonprofit organization and "donate" your desired expertise. Don't rely solely on your own intuition to research the right opportunity; seek the opinions of your colleagues and those who serve as your role models. You may find new open doors that might not have been apparent.

3. The network

Does the opportunity put you in touch with others who can help you achieve your personal purpose? Will this cause put you in touch with mentors, potential new clients, and friends?

You can build your network of influential, action-oriented achievers. Many workplaces lack the passion and collaboration that is often seen in volunteering for a nonprofit cause.

⇒   **Tip:**   Find out who serves on the agency's board and who are the volunteers who serve in key positions. Ask about the annual activities and regular working sessions to determine how often your presence will be required. Meetings and activities are opportunities to network and learn new leadership skills.

⇒   **Tip:**   In the words of author M. Scott Peck, "Collaboration is a way of working where both power struggles and excessive politeness take a back seat to team goals." You can experience the power of working cooperatively with other leaders who are cause-focused. You can gain collaboration skills and insights to bring back into your workplace.

"The biggest benefit I've received in giving to others is an enhanced understanding of the community in which I live," said one executive. "Volunteer service has enlarged my acquaintances and my perspectives. I have a much deeper understanding of people and the issues they confront. I am a more caring and compassionate person. Volunteerism has helped me value a diversity of ideas, cultures, and people in the community. It has added balance to my work life."

Assessing Nonprofit Agencies

If you are planning to develop the volunteering area of your CareerPortfolio, look for nonprofit agencies that demonstrate well-organized leadership. The agency should have a clearly articulated mission statement. Volunteers should have job descriptions and should be trained and recognized by the agency for making a difference. Volunteers should have input into the programs in which they serve.

---

4. Your ability to contribute

Does the opportunity give you an ability to contribute something of value? Does it enable you to gain professional recognition over time? Can you build your ability to solve problems and be accountable?

⇒ **Tip:** Productive and passionate volunteers can tell you exactly why they're volunteering. They know what they're contributing, and—just as important—what they're getting in terms of experiences gained and opportunities to contribute. The key is to match your volunteer position with your personal purpose.

5. Your available time

Does the time commitment fit with your schedule and lifestyle?

⇒ **Tip:** Find a volunteer situation that is compatible with your work schedule. If you work for an employer, ask for support in donating time to the worthy cause. Sell the benefits of the volunteer experience from your employer's point of view. The support of your employer plays a large role in your ability to volunteer during the work week.

⇒ **Tip:** If you face time constraints (for example, if you are a single parent with young children), you will need to find a suitable match that realistically addresses those limitations. In the above example, perhaps you could lead a youth program in which your children can participate.

Personal Journal...

Finding the right Volunteer Investment

1. List your personal purpose.

_____

_____

_____

_____

_____

_____

2. Write down the possible community causes that align with your personal purpose.

_____

_____

_____

_____

_____

_____

3. Describe the experiences you desire in order to grow your career wealth.

_____

_____

_____

_____

_____

_____

4. Describe the relationships you desire to develop to grow your career wealth.

_____

_____

_____

_____

_____

5. List your existing career skills and abilities that you can contribute today to this cause.

_____

_____

_____

_____

6. List possible ways to use your skills, such as delivering meals, writing news releases, lobbying officials on behalf of an organization, fund-raising, and so on.

_____

_____

_____

_____

_____

7. What Volunteer Investments are you already making?

_____

_____

_____

_____

8. What skills are you developing?

_____

_____

_____

_____

_____

9. Assess your available time. What might you need to give up in order to make a volunteering commitment?

_____

_____

_____

_____

_____

Making the time

You can tailor volunteerism to fit within your time constraints. Giving to others is a long-term investment. It should *not* be viewed as a liability or an expense. Because this is a voluntary pursuit, you can be selective. Although you cannot save the world, you can choose volunteer efforts that bring your business, your values, and your family together.

For example, Joyce, the Green Thumb (Chapter 4), was able to donate floral arrangements once a year to the annual town parade, plant roses outside of the city hall building, and be a guest speaker in her son's classroom. These were small ways in which she made a difference, and the payoff was huge: Joyce received public acknowledgments in local and school newspapers, and the extra publicity and new personal contacts helped her increase her business volume by 10 percent!

Remember that what's appropriate for one phase of your life may not be purposeful in the next. You might have once been able to spend several evenings a week in meetings for nonprofit agencies. Perhaps today you must be able to fit volunteerism into your business day once or twice a month, or look for occasional weekend opportunities.

> ➤ Many professionals prefer to donate evening hours to serve on boards of directors or to attend events where they can develop valuable networks with other executives.

> ➤ Many single parents are finding value in volunteering at their children's schools.

> ➤ Some people devote their time as leaders of their neighborhood's block watch programs.

Even young adults can gain tremendous career advantages through their Volunteer Investments.

Amanda Benthuysen is a college student who, by the age of 19, had spent 11 years as a volunteer. As National Youth Chairperson of the Muscular Dystrophy Association, Amanda has traveled across the country, speaking to audiences and meeting one-on-one with national dignitaries such as Secretary of State (then General) Colin Powell, helping to teach people about muscular dystrophy.

Amanda has muscular dystrophy, but that hasn't prevented her from taking on a volunteer role. Besides the personal sense of satisfaction, her high-profile role is preparing her for a lifetime of opportunities she may not otherwise have.

Volunteering can benefit stay-at-home parents

Even stay-at-home parents who have made the choice to reduce or eliminate a full-time job can keep skills alive and build new skills through volunteering.

"How to Profit From Volunteering," an article in *Parent* magazine's July 1998 issue, tells the story of Carolyn, who was an elementary school teacher before she stayed at home for 13 years to raise her children. She knew that she wanted to return to the workplace someday but wanted to try something new.

When her children were in preschool, Carolyn started volunteering and found that it was a great way to try out different types of jobs. Her first volunteer position, as a board member of a local parochial school, required about four hours each week, most of it spent reading at home to prepare for meetings. Later she raised funds for a center that helps children cope with the death of parents and siblings. When she was ready to return to work, Carolyn looked back on all of her volunteer experience and realized that what she really wanted to do was get a paying job related to children's health and education.

When she first re-entered the workplace at a California children's health council, Carolyn was in charge of a fund-raising campaign with a goal of $7 million. However, she was so successful that she raised a total of $9 million. Today she is the executive director for special gifts for a major university and medical center.

Personal Journal...

Making time for your Volunteer Investment

1. The available time that I can donate includes the following:

   Daytime: _____

   Evenings: _____

   Weekends: _____

2. The following arrangements, such as a discussion with my employer or baby-sitter, the help of my spouse or a family member, and so on, would need to occur in order for me to make the time:

   _____

   _____

   _____

   _____

   _____

3. List the action that you plan to take to explore the volunteer opportunity that best fits your personal purpose and available time.

Action _____

_____

_____

_____

By what date? _____

4. Answer the following questions:

What training opportunities are available to me if I want to learn specific new skills?

_____

_____

_____

_____

If I'm successful at my first tasks, where will my experience take me next?

_____

_____

_____

Is there someone in the organization who can act as an official or unofficial mentor to me?

_____

Am I comfortable with the organization's structure?

              Yes   No

Do I feel emotionally attached to the group?   Yes   No

Is the cause important to my ability to fulfill my personal purpose?

              Yes   No

Why do most people volunteer?

Most people volunteer because:

1. They were asked by someone.

2. They learned about the opportunity through an organization to which they belonged.

3. A family member or friend asked and would benefit as a result. In other words, many people volunteer to do their friends a favor, out of loyalty to the person requesting volunteer help.

Source: *U.S. News and World Report*, April 28, 1997.

Although these reasons may offer productive support, you may find that your Volunteer Investment may lack alignment with your personal purpose. If your underlying motivation is obligation, not purpose or passion, then it is likely that your Volunteer Investment payoff will be minimal.

If you are an executive, you may be appointed to serve on a number of boards and obligatory committees. As one bank vice president put it, he "ate a lot of chicken every week with people [he] didn't know." Although charity events are fun and beneficial, these functions can lack depth as a training ground for learning new career-oriented experiences.

Remember:

The role that volunteerism plays in your CareerPortfolio will depend on your personal purpose and the following factors:

➤ Your available time, based on priorities in your life (such as family responsibilities).

➤ Your ability to balance your priorities and integrate volunteerism in the most appropriate way.

➤ Career expertise that you desire to build.

➤ Your desire to make a difference in the world around you.

➤ Your age and stage in life.

➤ The value that you place on serving others.

Hedging career risk

Volunteer experiences can offer an important hedge to workplace career risk. When bosses know that their employees are respected in the community and have a strong network of supporters within and outside of the company, they are less likely to sabotage them. For example, Robert knew many influential political leaders due to his many years of volunteer work outside of his corporate setting. He was friends with his state's governor and many local leaders. One day, Robert's boss attempted to stir up some rumors and make him look incompetent. However, Robert had built a vast reserve of community credibility. The boss's moves backfired. None of the rumors circulated by the boss were believable, nor were they true. Upon hearing the rumor, Robert was able to tactfully confront his boss and use his network as a protective barrier against his boss's tricks.

Getting your employer's support

It's smart to let your employer know about your volunteer opportunities, responsibilities, and accomplishments. If you can show how your company will benefit from your added expertise, or prove that your role in the community will enhance your firm's ability to extend goodwill to the community and grow its connections within the community, gaining your employer's support may not be difficult. This assumes, of course, that you're a highly motivated employee and are viewed as adding value to your workplace.

In some cases, your company may support your efforts financially. Direct support from your employer may be needed if your volunteer activities occur during the business day or interfere with your business responsibilities.

Not all work environments are accepting of volunteerism during the day. In those cases, you will need to find an appropriate volunteer opportunity outside of your regular work time. However, many employers are starting to encourage volunteerism as a way to gain leadership expertise.

Getting on board

Serving on a board of directors can allow you to gain valuable management and decision-making skills as you assist an organization with important strategic and fiscal decisions.

When you're clear on what kind of leadership experience you want to gain, you don't have to know all of the ins and outs to get the process rolling. Getting on a board can be a simple process if you understand the basic steps:

> ➤ Know your personal purpose and expectations for joining a board of directors.

> ➤ Identify organizations that match your purpose and profile of expectations. Arrange for a tour of the organization, and have the agency staff send you information.

> ➤ Make sure you have the expertise it takes to join the board. Most boards seek professionals who are critical thinkers, who can weigh options and make good decisions. A financial or business background often is required to serve on for-profit as well as nonprofit boards.

> ➤ Tell colleagues who can help you connect with the organization. Once you've made your desires clear, you'll be surprised how your colleagues can provide advice and contacts you may not have access to on your own.

Personal Journal...
Balancing Volunteer Investments with life

1. Your personal purpose, your age and stage in life, your family responsibilities, your work responsibilities—all of these factors help you decide what you might be able to give when it comes to serving others. What kinds of expertise would you like to gain from a volunteer experience?

_____

_____

_____

2. Putting your priorities (your health, spouse, family, and financial well-being) first, what low-priority activity/activities might you be willing to give up in order to serve others?

    _____

    _____

    _____

3. Are you willing to go the extra mile to voluntarily support something you believe is important?   Yes   No

    If yes, how?

    _____

    _____

    _____

4. Are you willing to have a flexible or somewhat chaotic schedule every once in a while if that means the chance to give to others and learn and grow personally?   Yes   No

Volunteer Investments
in summary

➤ Know your personal purpose.

➤ Decide what kind of volunteer experience you need to obtain to build your desired CareerPortfolio.

➤ Brainstorm opportunities with colleagues. Use the five criteria mentioned on page 104 to gauge synergy with your personal purpose and your schedule. Compare your options and select the best one.

➤ Contact the organization you are interested in serving and find out the procedure for getting involved. Get support from your boss, if needed.

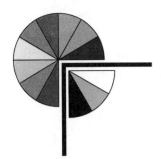

Chapter 7

Your Lifelong Learning Investments: Tools for Continual Growth

The fourth CareerPortfolio asset, made up of Lifelong Learning Investments, includes three powerful areas of focus for building your wealth of knowledge throughout your lifetime. These learning investments can pay off in your ability to retain your current job, get promoted, and keep pace with the rapidly changing global business environment. They include:

➤ Focused education.

➤ Focused reading.

➤ Mentorship (both being mentored and mentoring others).

Focused education

Focused education is an important part of growing your knowledge and skills. Formal courses and advanced degrees, workshops and seminars can protect you from becoming out-of-date and obsolete. Many forms of informal learning, such as self-directed research on the Internet, can also help you advance your skills and knowledge.

Building Lifelong Learning Investments into your schedule takes persistence and creativity. You must determine whether your sacrifice of time and energy will be worth the long-term payoffs. Remember, your next promotion may depend on your gaining certain types of knowledge.

Sam, the Busy Father of Four

After reaching vice-president status at a manufacturing trade association, Sam realized that his long-term goal was to develop children's software. To prepare for this direction, he determined he needed a four-year college degree, which became a major Lifelong Learning Investment. By putting himself on a fast track, spending two to three nights a week on campus, and cutting social activities with family and friends, he earned his computer information systems degree in three years.

"As a government affairs executive, I'm required to serve on community boards, which became an important part of my Volunteer Investment," Sam said. "My CareerPortfolio included information systems consulting on the side, based on computer expertise I had developed at other jobs."

"Information technology will present the best long-term opportunity to increase my income potential and do what I enjoy most. Going back to college was very challenging with four children under the age of 10. I worked late into the night and early mornings. Sometimes I felt like I was going crazy, but it was rewarding to finish this milestone," Sam said.

When he's not working or playing with his four children, Sam is developing educational software for children at night. This long-term dream will someday become his Primary Income Investment.

"I've made a pact with my oldest son that when I'm home, I'll limit my software development to one hour a day," Sam said. "My family is front and foremost. My CareerPortfolio is helping me support my family. My portfolio of expertise provides me with a great degree of freedom, knowing I am cultivating flexibility to provide for my family and create new career options that enhance family togetherness."

Sam's CareerPortfolio at-a-Glance

Sam's personal purpose—

To create interactive children's software that offers the user valuable educational benefits.

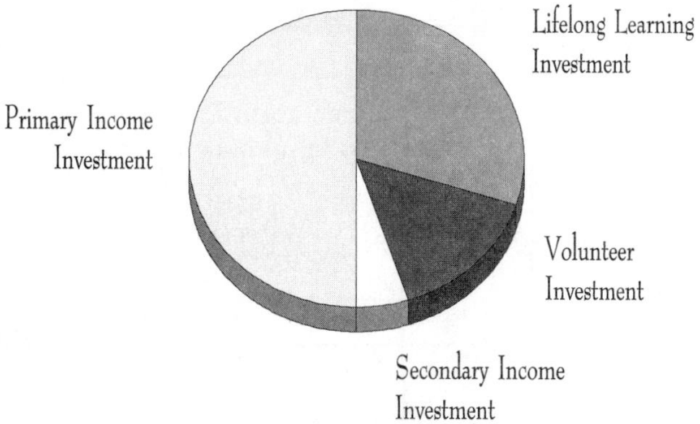
Lifelong Learning Investment
Primary Income Investment
Volunteer Investment
Secondary Income Investment

Primary $$$
- Government affairs vice president for trade association, representing a $2-billion statewide industry.

Secondary $$$
- Develops software on his own time at home.

Volunteer
- Numerous community boards and commissions.

Lifelong Learning
- Has mentors among high-tech colleagues.
- Mentors others; is sought out by those desiring information about technical and political content.

Educational Background and Former Jobs

Bachelor of Science degree in Computer Information Systems.

Steady promotions and a variety of industry and corporate experience.

Figure 23: Sam the Busy Father of Four

How does Sam do it?

Monday	Tuesday	Wednesday	Thursday	Friday	Saturday	Sunday
					Family Time	
Full-time work 8 a.m. to 5 p.m. Monday - Friday at trade						
association as lobbyist and government relations VP						
					One or two	
					clients per	
Attends volunteer community board meetings as part of business day.					month on	
					Saturdays.	
		Community/				
Family Time		civic outreach				
		once a week				
Late evening: Work on children's software					Work on children's software	

Figure 24: Sam's schedule

CareerPortfolio focused education tips

⇒ **Tip:** If you work in a large corporation, get on departmental mailing lists for relevant newsletters that promote workshops and events related to your field or personal purpose.

⇒ **Tip:** Call professional associations related to your CareerPortfolio and ask to be put on the mailing list for workshops and seminars.

⇒ **Tip:** Call local colleges or universities and request registration catalogs with course listings. Ask to be put on the college's mailing list.

Personal Journal...

Considering your education focus

1. Here are some questions to ask yourself as you consider work-shops and formal training:

   Is this a good fit with my work and family schedule? Yes   No

   How will an educational pursuit affect my current family, work, and leadership responsibilities?

   _____

   _____

   _____

   Can I rearrange or eliminate some of those responsibilities in order to focus on my educational pursuit?   Yes   No

2. Check your reasons for pursuing additional education, using the following list:

   _____ Interest in the subject at hand.

   _____ New opportunities will require additional education.

   _____ To be on a level playing field with peers, additional training/education is needed.

   _____ The hunger to learn and drive to complete the work.

   _____ A regimented workplace requirement.

   _____ Support/encouragement from a mentor, boss, or career counselor.

   _____ Other (describe).

   _____

   _____

   _____

   _____

Focused reading

Focused reading can help you stay on top of your career quickly, conveniently, and cost-effectively. To build career wealth, I recommend focusing your reading on the following areas (see Figure 25).

➤ Your purpose.

➤ Your field.

➤ Technology as relevant to your CareerPortfolio and achieving your personal purpose.

➤ Your personal finances.

➤ Positive thinking.

It's been said that if you study anything intensively for a year, you can become an expert at it! Reading is an inexpensive way to become self-taught in just about any subject matter. Readers tend to be leaders, because they're constantly growing their knowledge and can provide opinions and advice for the things that matter most.

Additionally, you can read to boost your financial savvy. By developing your financial knowledge and by building a financial nest egg, you'll be better prepared to try new career paths and take reasonable career risks that can help you fulfill your purpose.

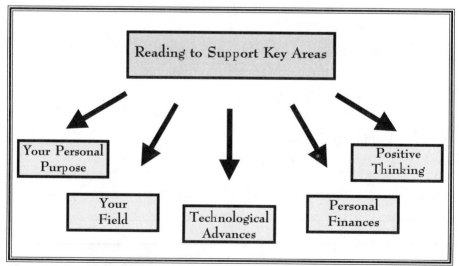

Figure 25: Reading to build your Lifelong Learning Investment

Focused reading tips

⇒   **Tip:**   **Set some measurable reading goals for specific topics or areas of learning.** For example, your goal might be to read one purpose-focused book per month about your personal purpose. At the end of the year, you'll have read 12 books and learned significantly more about achieving your purpose.

⇒   **Tip:**   **Read to provide leadership to others.** As a leader, you can pass learning along to others by reading and sharing worthwhile articles with your staff and colleagues.

⇒   **Tip:**   **Identify your most convenient (and cost-effective) reading resources.** Public libraries, university libraries, and corporate libraries can yield a gold mine of valuable reading, free of charge. If you're on a budget, the public library can be a wonderful resource.

⇒   **Tip:**   **Learn to use the Internet effectively for research.** Bookmark and frequently visit Web sites most valuable to your CareerPortfolio investments.

Personal Journal...
Integrating focused reading

In priority ranking, list your top three areas for learning through focused reading (for this year).

1. _____

2. _____

3. _____

Mentoring

Mentoring is a way to build (and impart) instant career wealth. Mentoring includes having and being a mentor, as well as using personal think tanks and creating your own "personal board of directors" to gain insight and input.

What is a mentor? Mentoring began in ancient times, when young boys were apprenticed to a master who excelled in a specific trade in order to learn from him. Today, a mentor is someone who takes an interest in your career and provides relevant encouragement.

A mentor is *not* a therapist, career savior, or buddy. For a healthy mentoring relationship to exist, an attitude of openness and a relationship of trust is critical between the mentor and the receiver of the information, the protégé. The most effective mentoring relationships involve win-win results for both the mentor and the protégé. More mentors today are expecting to gain valuable insights from those they mentor, or else the relationship may not be worth the time spent.

If you lack a formal mentor, don't be discouraged. You can search for various sources of mentoring. In fact, Marsha Sinetar, author of *The Mentor's Spirit: Life Lessons on Leadership and the Art of Encouragement,* promotes a fresh concept of mentoring. Rather than relying on one formal mentor, she advocates finding mentors in a variety of teachable moments, including letters, e-mail, tapes, teleconferences, and other informal ways of gaining fresh insight. With this approach, you can find "mentors" in everyday experiences and life's lessons, as well as from colleagues and people with whom you interact each day.

However, if you prefer the traditional adviser relationship, Sinetar advises:

1. The more emotionally needy you are, the less likely you'll be to attract top-level, productive mentors.

2. In all probability, the broader our mentors' responsibilities, the less personal time they'll devote to us.

3. The higher up your mentor is in his or her organization, the higher his or her expectations will be of your performance (and the more demands you'll need to place on yourself).

CareerPortfolio mentor tips

Where can you find a formal (or traditional) mentor relationship, in a world where most leaders are too busy with their own careers?

⇒ **Tip:** First, develop a short list of professionals you respect who have the following characteristics:

1. They are knowledgeable; considered by their peers to demonstrate superior achievement.

2. They have earned the respect of their colleagues by listening to, and communicating effectively with, others.

3. They recognize excellence in others and encourage it.

4. They demonstrate good judgment in decisions concerning themselves and the welfare of others.

5. They believe in the idea that there is plenty of success in life for *everyone;* opportunity and success are not scarce resources to be hoarded.

⇒ **Tip:** Know that your success as a protégé will depend on your bringing the following character traits to a mentoring relationship:

1. Willingness and openness to being coached. You may have heard the saying, "The athlete who trains himself is a fool." You must be willing to hear your mentors' advice.

2. Accountability. Once you receive advice from your mentors, you must be willing to be accountable for applying the advice by taking action and producing results.

3. Ability to contribute to the mentoring relationship. You need to make your relationships valuable, win-win situations for each of the people you identified.

⇒   **Tip:**   Once you've taken these steps, prioritize your list of possible mentors. Set up face-to-face meetings, beginning with your "top candidate," in which you discuss the possibility of forming a mentoring relationship for a set period of time. If your top candidate can't commit, then continue down the list until you find a good match.

1. Does this process feel too formal for your comfort zone? If so, choose one or more of the individuals you selected and consult informally with them on a periodic basis.

2. Define the areas in which you want to grow in order to achieve your personal purpose. Then be sure that these areas are addressed when you meet with your informal mentors.

3. Document the advice you receive and your progress in these areas over time. At the end of one year, you'll be amazed at how much wisdom you've absorbed, and applied, to your career pursuits.

Mentoring for professional development

According to the Society for Human Resource Management, many positive outcomes can result from workplace mentoring, including:

⇒ Performance excellence.

⇒ Self-confidence.

⇒ Organizational communication.

⇒ Creativity and idea exposure.

⇒ A cooperative, productive, service-oriented environment.

Personal Journal...

Finding your mentor

1. What kinds of advice would you like to gain through having a mentor?

_____

_____

_____

_____

_____

2. Who might be an ideal mentor for helping you achieve your personal purpose or helping you grow in certain areas?

_____

3. What kind of advice or reciprocal benefits can you offer to your mentor, adding value to the relationship?

_____

_____

_____

_____

You, the mentor

When you teach others what you know, you build your career wealth, too. That's because you take time to reflect, deepening your personal insight and conviction on a given subject. This kind of deep reflection and imparting of advice is one of the most rewarding aspects of mentoring others. If you help others achieve their dreams, not only will you benefit from teaching, you will position yourself as an admired leader in a world where selfish motives and a "me-first" attitude abound.

⇒ **Tip:** Be sure that if you agree to be a mentor to someone else you feel comfortable that the protégé is committed to learning from you.

⇒ **Tip:** Be sure that you can make the time commitment. For example, you may agree to provide advice in person once a quarter, or over the phone once a month. Make the arrangement workable for you.

Personal Journal...
Learning by mentoring others

1. What skills and wisdom do I already have that enable me to be a mentor to others?

_____
_____
_____
_____
_____
_____
_____
_____

2. Who has taught me lessons that I'd like to pass along to others?

_____
_____
_____
_____

3. What are five life lessons I'd like to share with others?

1) _____

_____

_____

2) _____

_____

_____

3) _____

_____

_____

4) _____

_____

_____

5) _____

_____

_____

Think tanks are an important learning resource

You may occasionally need some advice that requires creative group advice and collective thought. This is called a think tank. It's different from mentoring because you gather a number of ideas in a group session similar to a focus group. It's a fast and effective way to attack problems and gain fresh insights.

For example, if you are writing a book, you might gather a network of trusted professionals who can provide feedback on initial concepts. Or, you could seek ideas for developing your CareerPortfolio. For the small price of lunch, you can obtain advice and ideas that would have cost you thousands of dollars if you hired a consultant.

Facilitating a think-tank session

You can lead a think-tank meeting by selecting progressive, supportive colleagues and by gathering them via conference call or in person. On a monthly basis, you can facilitate personal and professional growth by using the following formula. Limit each participant's discussion to 15 minutes total. Cover the following three points:

1. **First five minutes:** The participant discusses accomplishments and insights. The participant must talk for no more than five minutes about what he or she has achieved in the past month—personally and professionally.

2. **Next nine minutes:** The participant shares career-related struggles and dilemmas, with a two-to-five-minute chance to discuss challenges. During this time, the group offers advice (similar to a corporate board) and encouragement (similar to a support group).

3. **The final minute:** Each person makes commitments that the group will help to reinforce during the next think tank.

Personal Journal...

Starting a think tank

Make a resource list of your best think-tank resources for your CareerPortfolio and for other projects. A table is provided below.

Type of issue or problem	Name of the think-tank resource

Lifelong Learning Investments
in summary

> ➤ Your Lifelong Learning Investments can protect you from becoming obsolete in the workplace.

> ➤ Align your learning investments with your personal purpose.

> ➤ Develop the right combination for your current circumstances of the following: formal and informal education, focused reading, and having and being a mentor.

> ➤ Try to read at least 15 minutes a day, focusing on topics that support your personal purpose.

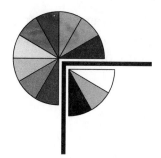

Chapter 8

CareerPortfolios for the Young, Old, and In-Between

No matter what age, you can live and work with purpose. As you journey toward your senior years, your CareerPortfolio investments will help you make the continuous transition to new pursuits. You can be a CareerPortfolio futurist by considering your senior years and planning CareerPortfolio investments that pay off for the long term, such as a hobby or volunteer pursuit.

America's massive baby-boomer generation already is redefining old age. Healthy seniors will attempt to work longer, and more seniors than ever will be living into their 90s, some reaching a centenarian birthday. Instead of becoming passive in senior life, millions of seniors will focus on reinventing the lives they have.

I want you to think of your CareerPortfolio as your tool for reinventing and re-calibrating your life work during your senior years. Proactively planning can help you address anxieties about aging, allowing you to focus your efforts on building a productive and purposeful life.

If you are a parent, you can use the CareerPortfolio as a planning tool to help your child leverage and build his or her special talents. You can have a profound impact on fostering your child's sense of purpose.

Jack, the Community Leader

Jack's CareerPortfolio began when he was a child and continued throughout his adulthood, bringing a lifetime of remarkable accomplishments. Jack's father, who owned a gas station in a rural town, died when Jack was only 3 years old. Jack's mother, a strong woman who was active in the community, was intent that her sons grow into boys of character, despite the unforeseen loss of their father.

"Some of the city's most prominent citizens took an interest in our well-being," Jack recalled. "I was raised by a strong, devoted mother, who had a deep sense of the value and importance of education. I also was mentored by a community of men who reached out to me with father-like guidance. My brother and I were, in a sense, children of the community. These were people who modeled a deep belief in community service and consensus building. This became a professional cornerstone," he said.

"In elementary school, I developed my sense of community responsibility as a volunteer crosswalk guard," Jack noted. "Even today I remember the pride and duty I felt."

As a young boy, Jack completed chores for a 20-cent per week allowance. In high school he helped support his mother and younger brother with summer jobs while playing football and excelling in math and science. His jobs included:

- Paper boy for the local newspaper.
- Bat boy for a men's softball team.
- Janitor in the county courthouse.
- Member of a survey crew for the state highway department.

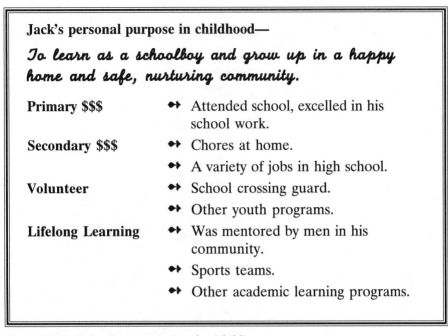

Jack's personal purpose in childhood—

To learn as a schoolboy and grow up in a happy home and safe, nurturing community.

Primary $$$	➼ Attended school, excelled in his school work.
Secondary $$$	➼ Chores at home.
	➼ A variety of jobs in high school.
Volunteer	➼ School crossing guard.
	➼ Other youth programs.
Lifelong Learning	➼ Was mentored by men in his community.
	➼ Sports teams.
	➼ Other academic learning programs.

Figure 26: Jack the Community Leader (child)

"My first recollection of patriotism began when my Cub Scout patrol was the color guard at a rally to sell war bonds during World War II. I stood at attention on a stage, holding the flag while the city fathers urged people to buy savings bonds. I knew I was part of something important, and it felt good," said Jack.

This mix of responsibility—academics, community giving, and summer jobs—would serve Jack well as a young adult.

Jack attended college and earned a degree in metallurgical engineering. After only one year working for a major oil company, Jack realized that he wanted to work more with people. Instead of spending years in a field that lacked the kind of interaction with people that he desired, he made the bold decision to return to school for a law degree. With his law degree, Jack:

➼ Became a partner in a large law firm.

➼ Was later hired by a large corporation and a few years later was promoted to general manager.

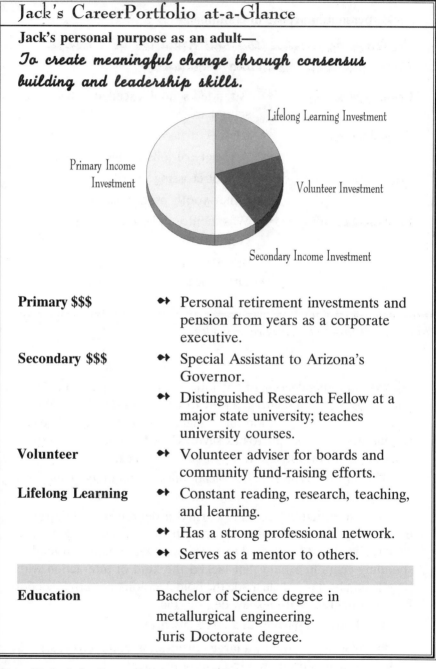

Jack's CareerPortfolio at-a-Glance

Jack's personal purpose as an adult—
To create meaningful change through consensus building and leadership skills.

Primary $$$	❧ Personal retirement investments and pension from years as a corporate executive.
Secondary $$$	❧ Special Assistant to Arizona's Governor.
	❧ Distinguished Research Fellow at a major state university; teaches university courses.
Volunteer	❧ Volunteer adviser for boards and community fund-raising efforts.
Lifelong Learning	❧ Constant reading, research, teaching, and learning.
	❧ Has a strong professional network.
	❧ Serves as a mentor to others.
Education	Bachelor of Science degree in metallurgical engineering. Juris Doctorate degree.

Figure 27: Jack the Community Leader (adult)

➻ Served on a number of national and local boards and commissions, where he contributed his legal and professional expertise. Through volunteerism, he further developed the art of finding collaborative solutions.

➻ Retired from the corporate world and was named a distinguished research fellow at a major university. Now in his 60s, he teaches at a state university and serves as an adviser to state government as well as to nonprofit associations.

"Setting difficult, yet achievable, personal objectives motivates me to constantly upgrade my skills," Jack said. "My diversity of business and community friends and their perspectives provided me with a much deeper understanding of people and the issues they confront."

How does Jack do it?

Monday	Tuesday	Wednesday	Thursday	Friday	Saturday	Sunday
9 a.m to 5 p.m. Business, learning, and community service/volunteer activities are intergrated.					Relaxation, reading, hobbies, and down time.	
	Occasional evenings: civic/social events.					

Figure 28: Jack's schedule

Personal Journal...

Planning for senior years

Answer the questions below. There are no right or wrong answers, so think creatively!

1. What will you be like when you're age 65 and older? Select one-word descriptions that will most likely describe you. Or, circle words below that may help to describe you in your mature years.

Stately	Adventuresome
Earthy	Traveling
Fashionable	Humorous
Eccentric	Inspiring
Relaxed	On-the-go

    Others? List here.

    _____

    _____

    _____

    _____

    _____

2. Glimpsing ahead, brainstorm your ideal personal purpose statement for your senior years (65 and older) or things that will mean the most to you at that stage of life (based on what you think today).

    _____

    _____

    _____

    _____

    _____

Why you need a CareerPortfolio for your senior years

➤ In the United States, 10,000 people turn 50 every day. Seniors in their 80s and beyond will be the fastest growing population during the next 50 years, according to demographic studies. Because of the advances in medicine and health technology, senior citizens will be living longer. Those who plan for a purposeful senior life are better equipped to ensure that they fulfill their purpose.

➤ More than 120 million baby boomers and post-boomers are moving toward their senior years. Will they be optimistic and excited about what the future brings, driven by confidence that life has purpose? Or will they be fearful and hopeless?

Lydia Bronte, a psychologist who conducted a 1998 Carnegie Corporation study of 150 actively employed senior citizens between the ages of 65 and 101, found that "The single most important element to developing a long career, or creating an active post-retirement life, is to find meaningful and fulfilling work that keeps you engaged and happy, whether paying or nonpaying." Flexibility, adaptability, and a refusal to stay too long at work they didn't enjoy were all advantages for the active seniors she studied.

➤ It is predicted that in the United States, the majority of those who reach age 65 will not be able to retire because of financial need and the high probability that Social Security will not exist. As significant, most of these younger senior citizens *will not want to retire*. Retiring at age 65 is not a productive goal for those who find personal satisfaction in using their skills and gifts to fulfill a purpose.

➤ Keeping your learning edge and using your brain are significant factors that contribute to vital and vigorous aging. Recent brain research is proving that as people learn new things, brain synapses continue to grow inside the brain, leading to continued alertness.

Personal Journal...
Describing your senior CareerPortfolio

What would you like your CareerPortfolio to look like in your senior years? Draw it below, based on what you visualize today. Include asset areas that may be applicable for your situation, and describe each.

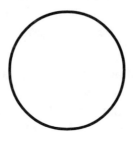

Primary Income Investment:

_____

_____

_____

Secondary Income Investment:

_____

_____

_____

Volunteer Investment:

_____

_____

_____

Lifelong Learning Investment:

_____

_____

_____

A Day in the Life of Cheryl the Doctor, an Active Senior Citizen

Here's how an active senior citizen might implement the CareerPortfolio approach:

Upon retirement, Cheryl, a former family physician, shifted from an on-site job to an online fulfillment of her purpose. She wakes up at a leisurely 8 a.m. and logs on to the Internet for her highly customized news service. She downloads articles onto her computer **(Lifelong Learning)**. After scanning the news, Cheryl has breakfast and plans her day.

First, she sends an e-mail to her political representatives and advocates a bill to educate young people about the hazards of smoking **(Volunteer)**. Then she updates her personal home page and answers readers' e-mails **(Volunteer)**.

Cheryl then completes her freelance column for a medical trade journal, which she e-mails to her editors **(Secondary Income)**.

Following lunch, Cheryl conducts stock investment transactions over the Web. Her 401(k) investment plan **(Primary Income)**, cultivated from years spent in her medical practice, now provides a comfortable income.

Cheryl spends the remainder of the afternoon making phone calls to catch up with friends. She and her husband finish the day by meeting friends for dinner.

The KidsPortfolio

As a parent, you can use the CareerPortfolio model to help encourage your child to develop a number of character-building interests that pay off as he or she becomes an adult. You can help your children take personal responsibility for developing a variety of skills and interests that someday will result in a resilient CareerPortfolio and many new opportunities.

The KidsPortfolio parallels the CareerPortfolio. It features four major investment areas that can help your child develop a well-balanced portfolio of learning experiences. See Appendix H for specific ideas that support each area of the KidsPortfolio.

KidsPortfolio Asset	Parallel to CareerPortfolio
Academics: The opportunity to learn and earn good grades at school comes first.	**Primary Income Investment**
Chores and Allowance: The opportunity to earn an allowance by completing chores.	**Secondary Income Investment**
Volunteer Investment: The opportunity to develop concern for others and to gain experience by helping others.	**Volunteer Investment**
Hobbies and Role Models: The opportunity to build an area of unique giftedness and be inspired by a mentor or role model.	**Lifelong Learning Investment**

Why your child needs a KidsPortfolio

> ➤ In the future, it will no longer be enough to learn a trade and practice it for the rest of your life. To stay competitive, workers will be required to be learning professionals. Learning won't stop after the college degree, because professionals will need to analyze and apply new information to each and every project.

> ➤ Continuous learning will help your child address four areas of his or her life: the need to keep up with accelerated knowledge requirements; the opportunity to continually strengthen the mind; career development; and the ability to continue to reach goals.

> ➤ The value of taking personal responsibility over one's career begins early in life. As children discover they have something valuable to offer, they know they belong. They can begin to view themselves as worthwhile members of a unit—a family, a classroom, a neighborhood, and a community.

> ➤ To adapt to an ever-changing workplace, students will need to be flexible, fast learners, able to shift directions and adapt to and master new technology.

Personal Journal...
Purpose as the foundation

You can help your child gain helpful insights into a personal purpose statement appropriate for his or her stage in life. Some of the following questions may be helpful to pose to your child.

1. If you could do anything you'd want to, what would that be?

_____

_____

_____

_____

2. What are you doing when you're having the most fun?

_____

_____

_____

_____

3. When do you feel closest to your family?

_____

_____

_____

_____

To your friends and neighbors?

_____

_____

_____

4. If you could do something to help someone else, what would that be?

_____

_____

_____

_____

5. What are some of the things you do best?

_____

_____

_____

_____

6. What do you consider your biggest accomplishments?

_____

_____

_____

_____

7. Which activities do you enjoy the most?

_____

_____

_____

_____

8. What is your favorite class in school?

_____

Why? _____

_____

_____

9. What career choices have you considered?

_____

_____

_____

What are the benefits?

_____

_____

_____

The risks?

_____

_____

_____

Then help your child draft a personal purpose statement. Talk it over with your child. If needed, help the child revise it until he is satisfied that it describes his ideas. Post it somewhere, such as in the child's room. Help the child develop a KidsPortfolio, pointing out how each activity helps to support the child's personal purpose statement.

Steps for creating a KidsPortfolio

Help your child develop a KidsPortfolio by taking the following steps:

1. Get your child involved with creating his or her own personal purpose statement. Use the questions posed earlier in this chapter as a guide.

_____

_____

_____

_____

2. Analyze the ingredients that currently exist in your child's portfolio, and map the ingredients out by using the empty pie chart that follows.

Current

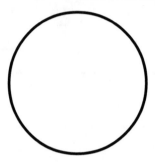

3. Consider asset areas that may be missing. How might you encourage your child to consciously integrate that ingredient, such as a Volunteer Investment, into his or her routine? (It could be something that occurs only once or twice a year.)

Desired

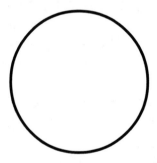

4. Create an action plan for integrating one or more elements of the KidsPortfolio into your child's life.

5. Monitor your child's investments quarterly. Make changes as needed.

CareerPortfolios for all ages
in summary

> No matter what your age, you can live and work with purpose.

> You can be your child's greatest source of inspiration for finding purpose in his or her young life. You can help your child build a simple portfolio of diverse skills, commitments, and interests.

> Your senior years can bring great enjoyment and satisfaction in using your skills and interests to make a difference in your world. It's never too late to build a CareerPortfolio. Your unique, purposeful legacy is still to be written!

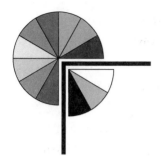

Chapter 9

Building Your CareerPortfolio: A 12-Month Guide

Within the first few months of reading this book, you can make significant progress toward building your CareerPortfolio. By making investments
in at least two of the four career assets, you can begin to steadily increase
your career rewards and reduce career risk within 12 months.

This chapter provides a month-by-month guide to help you begin your
CareerPortfolio action plan. These steps allow plenty of room for personal flexibility so that you can tailor your own unique plan. For example,
you might aggressively address all four areas of your CareerPortfolio within
12 months. Or, you may want to concentrate your efforts on pursuing a
new Primary Income Investment. This could require a significant amount
of focused time and energy. (In this case, a two-year plan may be more
realistic.)

Here is an overview of the basic 12-month plan.

First Quarter: Focus on Primary Income Investment.

Second Quarter: Focus on Secondary Income Investment.

Third Quarter:	Focus on Lifelong Learning. (This provides a time for reflection and growth.)
Fourth Quarter	Focus on Volunteer contributions, to assess and either create or redirect your volunteer efforts.
End of the Year	Conduct end-of-the-year assessment. Start over with continual assessment and check-up plan.

Note: If a job change is required for your Primary Income Investment, spend both the first and second quarters focusing on your new job. Resume the basic plan in the third quarter with Lifelong Learning and finish the year as stated. If you begin a new Primary Income Investment, I do not recommend that you attempt to integrate a Secondary Income Investment in the same year. Whatever your pace, the most important step is, simply, to begin the process of making purposeful investments.

Once your CareerPortfolio begins to take shape, you may want to showcase your expertise through use of a Life Experience Resume. This type of resume takes all of your relevant career-related experiences (whether for pay or volunteer-based) and spotlights the assets in a meaningful way.

A 12-month plan:
Practical steps for building your CareerPortfolio

First quarter:
Building alignment around your purpose

During the first quarter, you should gain a solid understanding of your personal purpose—your unique reason for being—and begin to map out a desired set of CareerPortfolio assets. Then you will focus on your Primary Income Investment, putting the most immediate focus on assessing how your major source of income can help you achieve your personal purpose in an even more rewarding way.

Month 1: Creating your ideal CareerPortfolio

Week 1: Personal Purpose

Draft your personal purpose. Use the exercises in Chapter 3 to guide you through the process. Revisit your working draft several times during the week to refine and reaffirm your purpose statement.

Week 2: Identify existing assets and gaps

Assess your current CareerPortfolio asset areas by completing the pie chart exercise on page 31. Map out both your existing and desired allocation of career assets (Primary Income Investment, Secondary Income Investment, Volunteerism, and Lifelong Learning).

1. Assess whether your current career asset allocations align with your purpose.

2. Note discrepancies between your existing and desired CareerPortfolio.

3. Prioritize the career assets you want to develop, ranking them from most urgent to least urgent. For example, you may determine that developing a Secondary Income Investment is your highest priority. Under that asset, you would list, in order of importance, the discrepancies that exist. For example, you may be lacking a personal purpose. In this case, you would plan some action steps that help you discover your purpose and options for career paths that support your purpose. One of the action steps in this case might be to meet with a career consultant or a human resources professional at your company who can spend some time helping you find your niche.

Week 3: Plan for reaching your desired state in 12 months

Now that you've assessed the current state of your CareerPortfolio and your areas of immediate priority, it's time to map your desired state for each CareerPortfolio asset, envisioning what you would like to achieve after 12 months (see Figure 29).

Career Area	Desired State 12 Months from Today	Benefits	Gaps Noted	Action Needed in this CareerPortfolio Asset Area	By When?
Primary Income Investment					
Secondary Income Investment 1					
2					
3					
4					
5					

Figure 29: Mapping your desired state (Continued on page 155)

Career Area	Desired State 12 Months from Today		Benefits	Gaps Noted	Action Needed in this CareerPortfolio Asset Area	By When?
Volunteer Investment	1					
	2					
	3					
	4					
	5					
Lifelong Learning Investment						

Figure 29 (cont'd.): Mapping your desired state

➤ Assess your Primary Income Investment according to how well it helps you accomplish your personal purpose. List your desired state 12 months from now. Develop your action steps and deadlines for accomplishing those steps.

➤ Develop a list of three to five potential Secondary Income Investment sources that use your existing skills and align with your personal purpose. With this in mind, list the desired state for your Secondary Income Investment.

➤ Develop a list of three to five volunteer pursuits that would help you fulfill your personal purpose, and get a contact name and number in each organization with whom you could meet.

➤ Develop a goal for your Lifelong Learning area for the current calendar year.

Week 4: List those who can help you in the next 12 months

Identify a mentor or mentors who can assist you with achieving your personal purpose, or who can help you address the gaps you've listed. Select people who excel in the areas you'd like to develop, people who can provide you with valuable advice throughout the year. Contact your mentor (by phone, by e-mail, or in person by appointment, based on what works best), and let him or her know about your plans to pursue a CareerPortfolio. Explain that you'll be contacting him or her periodically for advice.

Gap Area	Name of Mentor	Phone Number
_____	_____	_____
_____	_____	_____
_____	_____	_____
_____	_____	_____
_____	_____	_____
_____	_____	_____
_____	_____	_____

Month 2: Seek purpose in your Primary Income Investment

Week 1: Assess Primary Income Investment alignment

Before you address other gap areas, be sure that your Primary Income Investment goes well with your CareerPortfolio. Reread Chapter 4 and complete the exercises. Note that your CareerPortfolio can help you assess promotions and new opportunities within your current company, too. For example, some promotions may not support your personal purpose, even if they offer a higher salary. You can weigh the pros and cons of taking a position that does not align with your personal purpose, and that may in fact prevent you from establishing your CareerPortfolio.

Week 2: Look to enhance your purpose through your Primary Income Investment

How can your Primary Income Investment help you achieve your personal purpose in a more fulfilling way? You may not need to find a new job. You may be able to explore fresh new ways to fulfill your purpose through your Primary Income Investment to achieve certain features of your personal purpose. For example, if you want to be a leading-edge teacher, perhaps you need to develop ways to share lessons learned from your department's projects in staff meetings and with your peers on the job.

Do the following exercise during the week:

1. How can you maximize your personal purpose through:

    ⇒ Technical expertise and excellence?

    ⇒ Friendships and work relationships on the job? (This could include learning from others and teaching and encouraging others, including colleagues, your customers, your superiors, and your subordinates.)

2. Contact your mentor. Ask your mentor how he or she accomplishes a personal purpose through a Primary Income Investment.

3. Determine and document your next steps here based on the above answers.

Weeks 3 and 4: Career counseling and testing: Is change on the horizon?

Note: If you need to change your Primary Income Investment, use months 2 and 3 to focus on your change. Reread Chapter 5. You may need an additional few months to make the desired changes in your life. If so, skip to the Second Quarter activities when you're ready to proceed.

Now that you've conducted a personal assessment, explore the career resources within your company's human resources department. Are there career counseling services available? If not, you may want to seek the advice of a professional career counselor through an executive search firm, or by visiting your local university's career services center. Many career assessments can help you discover your aptitudes, your driving performance characteristics, and your work style.

Month 3: Launch your job search

If your Primary Income Investment strategy is to change jobs, use this month to conduct a job search. This may include visiting with contacts at your current company, deciding if you're ready to start your own business, or contacting executive recruiters to find work elsewhere.

(If your Primary Income Investment strategy is to start your own business, go to the Second Quarter activities.)

Weeks 1 through 4:

Continue career testing if needed. Begin searching your professional networks and associations. Contact executive search firms, if applicable. Contact your professional association job hotline, if applicable. Scan the newspapers for opportunities; however, recognize that as many as 90 percent of all jobs come through informal networking, not newspaper employment listings.

Personal Journal...
First Quarter Notes

_____

_____

_____

_____

_____

_____

_____

_____

_____

_____

_____

_____

_____

_____

_____

_____

_____

_____

_____

_____

_____

_____

_____

_____

Second quarter:
Establishing your Secondary Income Investment

Note: If you change your Primary Income Investment, I recommend that you take another three months to settle into your new Primary Income Investment role, due to the focus and energy a new job requires. While you settle into your new job, skip to the Third Quarter activities—Lifelong Learning—which can immediately boost your Primary Income Investment learning.

Month 4: Consider your potential Secondary Income Investment

Week 1: Exploring Options

Complete the exercises in Chapter 5. This will give you an idea of what kind of business you may want to start and what kind of time you have available.

Based on your skills and interests, gather a few friends and have the group help you brainstorm a project or a business that you may want to pursue to provide the experience of gaining a Secondary Income Investment. For example, if you currently are an administrative assistant in a corporate office, perhaps you could help entrepreneurs organize a database or their office space. If you are an architect, perhaps you could provide occasional consulting expertise outside of your design work by providing advice to homeowners on how to maximize their living space.

Week 2: Get ideas and legal advice

Contact mentors who have started their own businesses. Ask questions and gather input.

Read *The Small Business Start-Up Guide,* by Robert Sullivan. This book is a one-stop bank of valuable information, with state-by-state resources for establishing a business, no matter how small or big.

Consider your business's legal structure. Will it be a sole proprietorship, a partnership, or a corporation? If it will be a corporation, which kind will it be: a C-corporation, an S-corporation, or limited liability corporation? Contact an attorney to begin discussing the legal framework of your business and how much it will cost to file the necessary documents. (More legal work will be done in weeks to come; this is just a beginning.)

Week 3: Research your ideas to assess market potential

Begin your business plan with preliminary research. Describe your desired product or service based on what you'd like to be doing. Document existing competitors who already provide that product. At what price do your competitors sell the product or service?

Week 4: Define your product or service and your market

Think about your product or service. Describe your targeted customers. What are their wants and needs? If you don't know, begin to ask around, starting with your friends and people who use this kind of product or service. If needed, refine your definition of what you'll offer with the feedback you receive.

Month 5: Implementing a Secondary Income Investment

Week 1: Define your supplies and determine your financing

Determine what kind of supplies you will need to run your business. List supplies and big-ticket items on a month-by-month basis for the first 12 months to give yourself a realistic look at your first year. (See the business startup check list in Appendix I.)

Describe what kind of money or financing will be needed, if any. There are plenty of books in the library about starting a business and obtaining financing if needed. The Small Business Administration (SBA) is great resource for information, including SBA's Senior Corps of Retired Executives, or SCORE.

List your sources for financing (bank loan, credit card, family member, and so on). Determine your plan of action if you need to obtain financing. Hire an accountant, if needed, to help you put together a proposal for funding.

Week 2: Finalize your business plan

Finish your business plan, putting together all of the written exercises you've documented since the beginning of Month 4. By now, your summary of exercises should flow like a business plan.

Weeks 3 and 4: Finalize the legal structure, logo, and brand image

Using a creative resource such as a graphic artist, or an advertising agency if necessary, develop your business logo and name. Determine what image, or "brand personality," you desire when people see your logo. Complete the following statement:

"When people see my logo, they will think of _____

_____

_____ .

Unlike my competitors, my company will be known for _____

_____

_____ ."

I suggest that you focus on one of the following areas: customer focus; operational excellence; or low cost. Do not try to be all three; outstanding companies focus on one of the above areas and excel in that area.

Now that you have researched your options for business structures, establish the legal structure for your business. You may want to hire an attorney to assist you in developing and filing your company's legal framework with the appropriate local, state, and federal entities. This includes establishing yourself as a corporation, filing for patents and trademarks, and so on. A certified public accountant (CPA) is an ideal resource for providing you with tax advice.

Month 6: Financing your business

Weeks 1 and 2: Secure financing, if needed

Explore and obtain the financing you need to get you through your first year of business.

Begin to buy some of the supplies you need to get started. Do not over-buy! You will need to be careful to balance your outflow of cash with your inflow of revenue from business operations. Remember, the revenue will lag behind your expenses. Do not spend too much of your newly created capital, or you may not be able to pay your bills (suppliers, office expenses, and so on).

Finish your logo's design, now that you have given ample thought to your business and what it represents.

Weeks 3 and 4: Continue to develop your operational plan and implement tactics

Develop back-office procedures, such as database management, billing, and record keeping. Hire an accountant if needed, for financial record keeping and tax purposes.

Print business cards; set up a fax machine. Begin to build a customer prospecting list, if applicable.

Third Quarter:
Continuing momentum with Lifelong Learning Investments

Personal Journal...
Second Quarter Notes

_____

_____

_____

_____

_____

_____

_____

Second Quarter Notes(cont'd.)

_____

_____

_____

_____

_____

_____

_____

_____

_____

Months 7 through 9: Learn by studying and talking to people

Use the next three months to become a student of topics and people relating to your Primary Income Investment, your Secondary Income Investment, and your personal purpose. This could include reading, attending workshops, inviting a think-tank group to lunch, and seeking advice from your mentor(s).

If you have landed a new Primary Income Investment, use these months to study areas related to your new job or business. If you have recently integrated a Secondary Income Investment, study in areas relevant to conducting a successful business. If you have both Primary and Secondary Income Investments in place and are satisfied with them, you may want to focus your learning on areas relevant to Volunteerism.

Personal Journal...
Third Quarter Notes

_____

_____

_____

_____

_____

_____

_____

_____

_____

_____

_____

_____

_____

_____

_____

_____

_____

_____

_____

_____

_____

_____

_____

_____

_____

_____

_____

_____

_____

_____

Fourth Quarter: Pursuit of a volunteer asset and year-end review

Month 10: Matching Volunteerism with your Personal Purpose

Week 1: Assess potential opportunities right for you

Complete the exercises in Chapter 7. If you are not currently volunteering in a capacity that aligns with your personal purpose, decide on one volunteer project or organization that can help you do this. Contact the organization and request an informational interview with the person who works with volunteers. This is an excellent way to network, learn about a new field, and gain access to what would normally be a closed circle. Although your visit is non-threatening, you are positioning yourself for future opportunities that may crop up.

Weeks 2 through 4: Narrow your field of opportunities

Take a tour of the agency you are interested in and arrange follow-up visits if necessary. After investigating volunteer opportunities, determine the volunteer opportunity that will best enable you to meet your personal purpose. Follow up with the agency's director and schedule a time to get acquainted with your new volunteer role. Learn all you can about the agency's mission, board, and committees, and meet other volunteers.

Month 11: Settling into the volunteer role

Weeks 1 through 4:

Continue to find your niche in the volunteer agency. Note your progress, challenges, and next steps.

Month 12: Year-end review

Week 1:

Complete a year-end assessment. Revisit your personal purpose (and Chapter 2). Draw your portfolio as it stands today. Think about the year ahead, and draw the portfolio you wish to have 12 months from now. Note the experiences and skills you'd like to achieve, and consider ways to obtain them. For example, perhaps you are a new manager but lack people skills. Your CareerPortfolio ingredients should reflect opportunities where you can gain people skills.

Week 2:

Update your resume, integrating your new career assets.

Weeks 3 and 4:

Review your CareerPortfolio and update your plans for future investments. Use this 12-month model as a tool to continually plan each area of your CareerPortfolio. Repeat the exercises in this book to continue refining and building your career assets. Most important, determine your major new steps for the year ahead. Some years may not require much change. Other years may bring major adjustments as your life circumstances change.

Personal Journal...
Fourth Quarter Notes

_____

_____

_____

_____

_____

_____

Fourth Quarter Notes (cont'd.)

Annual monitoring

Ever since I began my career, I've used the New Year's holiday as a time to evaluate my career as well as other areas of my life. I encourage you to celebrate the successes of your past year, as well as to set goals and dreams for the year ahead.

Looking back provides a sense of closure and thankfulness for the many lessons learned. It can allow you to view the year in the context of a bigger picture. By developing a road map for the year ahead, you can begin a fresh new year knowing that your updated CareerPortfolio will continue to support your Personal Purpose.

Personal Journal...
Annual Notes

_____

_____

_____

_____

_____

_____

_____

_____

_____

_____

_____

_____

_____

_____

_____

_____

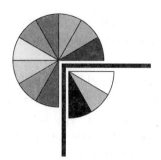

Afterword

Final Thoughts: Being a CareerPortfolio Futurist

Congratulations! You've made great progress in creating exciting and purposeful possibilities for your future. You are well on your way to finding new purpose in your career. Just as important, you will consciously plan the kinds of career investments that will help you achieve this truly unique and wonderful purpose intended just for you.

Take the time to complete the Personal Journals and exercises in Appendix H. That way, you can continue the journey of self-discovery that will bring joy and personal fulfillment as you continue to develop your next steps. You will begin to custom fit your career investments to your personal purpose, with a thorough understanding of why you're making those investments. Refer back to these valuable exercises once a year, or as you feel the need to explore your career direction. I recommend that you review your CareerPortfolio at least once a year to reassess your career investments and make adjustments as needed.

Let me hear from you. Send me an e-mail at *cp@careerportfolio.net*, and visit my Web site, *www.careerportfolio.net,* for more CareerPortfolio ideas.

Remember, you are a unique and special person created for a unique purpose. I wish you great success as you plan and implement your CareerPortfolio. May your career-related investments bring purpose and satisfaction to every area of your personal life, and may you leave behind a purposeful legacy to the precious people in your life.

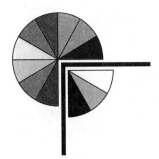

Appendix A

The CareerPortfolio Investment Profile

The first step in considering your CareerPortfolio is to identify:

1. Your career risk tolerance.

2. Your career objectives.

3. Your career time horizon.

Complete the CareerPortfolio Investment Profile. In the right-hand column for each question, circle the number of the response that best matches your career philosophy and goals. Based on this information, you will score the results, and begin to discover the CareerPortfolio mix of assets most appropriate for you. Revisit this assessment every two to three years to stay in touch with your changing career needs.

Risk Tolerance

You have just been given a windfall of five hours a day! How would you invest it?

I would invest it only at the place where I currently work.	1
I would invest it in a meaningful activity other than my work that offers at least one benefit (such as a high profile, a good reputation, or fame), as long as it came with only a moderate amount of career risk.	2
I would invest it in at least three other meaningful ways that offered significant gains of experience, reputation, and advancement potential with a moderate amount of risk.	3
I would select a mix of career-related activities that offer considerable new and exciting experiences with a high amount of probable risk, such as a risky new business that could afford fun opportunities and potentially lots of income.	4

Which of the following statements best describes your probable reaction if your schedule suddenly seemed overwhelming to maintain?

I would be very concerned because I cannot accept interruptions or stress at my job, my family life, or anything else right now.	1
If my current job or business is unaffected, it would not bother me.	2
I already invest for long-term career growth, but would be concerned if I seemed overwhelmed.	3
I invest for long-term career growth and accept fluctuations in my time demands and personal schedule.	4

Which of the following CareerPortfolio investments would you feel most comfortable pursuing?

Refining my job, or Primary Income Investment, to match my personal purpose.	**1**
Taking classes or obtaining an advanced degree related to my personal purpose.	**2**
Pursuing a volunteer activity to gain new and needed experience.	**3**
Starting a business.	**4**

How optimistic are you about the long-term prospects for your career?

Negative.	**1**
Unsure.	**2**
Somewhat positive.	**3**
Very optimistic.	**4**

Risk tolerance total _____

Your CareerPortfolio Investment Objectives

Which is most important to you?

The safety of my current job or business I own.	1
The amount of self-confidence and personal reward generated by understanding and pursuing my personal purpose.	2
Increasing my self-confidence and my income potential.	3
Increasing my overall career wealth over the long term, so that I will have a high degree of flexibility and numerous skills even when I'm in my senior years.	4

Which of the following best describes your CareerPortfolio investment objectives?

Preserving/protecting my current job or business I own.	1
Growing my skill base.	2
Growing my skill base and getting promoted (or growing my business).	3
Growing both my experience base and my flexibility to switch careers, and enhancing my variety of career experiences over an extended time frame.	4

You expect that five years from now your career will be:

More dissatisfying, boring, or worse than now.	1
The same as now.	2
Somewhat better than now in terms of enjoyment, options, flexibility, and personal benefits.	3
Substantially better than now in terms of enjoyment, options, flexibility, and personal benefits.	4

The safety of your Primary Income Investment, in terms of developing your CareerPortfolio is:

A primary concern.	**1**
Fairly important.	**2**
Not important.	**3**

What do you want to do with the benefits you receive from your CareerPortfolio?

Get promoted.	**1**
Get promoted, and step up in leadership and responsibility, whether it be on the job or in the community.	**2**
Become so successful that I have more time to spend on the right combination of career assets that are meaningful to me and allow me to help others.	**3**

CareerPortfolio investment objectives total _____

Time Horizon

How old are you?

56 and above	1
46 to 55	2
36 to 45	3
20 to 35	4

What is your primary CareerPortfolio goal?

Job preservation.	1
Learning.	2
Learning and helping others.	3
Being the best possible steward of my time and talents, and preparing for change and the ability to be flexible later in life.	4

What is the time frame for you to achieve your CareerPortfolio goals?

0 to 5 years	1
5 to 10 years	2
10 years or longer	3

Time horizon total _____

Investor Profile Analysis with Adjusted Totals

(The total for each section of the profile is weighted; that is, multiplied by a factor that represents its overall importance in choosing a CareerPortfolio.)

Risk Tolerance total _____ x 3 = _____

Investment Objectives total _____ x 2 = _____

Time Horizon total _____ x 1 = _____

Total _____

Suggested CareerPortfolio Asset Allocation	Adjusted Total	Recommended Action Steps
Conservative	27 to 52	Even if you are conservative in your career approach, you need some diversification to offset career risk (such as layoffs, mergers, and skills becoming obsolete). Consider adding one CareerPortfolio asset in addition to your Primary Income Investment. As you begin to feel more comfortable with your diversified CareerPortfolio, consider other investments.
Balanced	46 to 81	You are likely to do well with at least three CareerPortfolio assets, and are able to balance work, family, and your investments.
Aggressive	73 to 108	You need a challenge and are stimulated by a variety of pursuits. You should most likely go after all four CareerPortfolio assets and discover the mix that works well for you. As you move forward in life, you will reallocate your time and energy, focusing on what's most important.

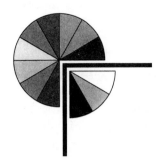

Appendix B

Career Risk and Your Time Horizon

Your life stage (time horizon) and your tolerance for career risk will affect your CareerPortfolio decisions. For example, if you are in your late 60s, you may want to concentrate your time and energy on Volunteer Investments rather than develop a new Secondary Income Investment.

Risk tolerance measures the amount of risk you are willing to accept for expanding your career investments beyond your one job. It takes guts to begin a business venture, invest in a learning opportunity, or get involved in a volunteer project. Only you can determine your desire to reach beyond your comfort zone.

With your personal purpose, your life stage, and your tolerance for risk in mind, only you can determine your best use of time and what you are willing to give up in order to build a career asset. CareerPortfolios must be tailored to fit our ever-evolving life circumstances.

Assessing your risk tolerance

Your CareerPortfolio can help you at any stage of your career life. It is important to recognize that each of us has differing abilities for integrating people and projects into our lives. Also, your capacity to maintain two to four areas of your CareerPortfolio may change over time. The chart on pages 183 and 184 provides an example of how one might interpret a CareerPortfolio in life stages, acknowledging many of the common traits noted in a person's life cycle.

Understanding the general characteristics of life and career changes can enable you to consider the kinds of career investments that are most appropriate, based on your purpose, your available time, and your tolerance for accepting the risk of taking on new career investments. By developing the right investments, you can prepare for an uncertain future. Instead of worrying about turning points that exist in life, you can make CareerPortfolio investments that help you build new career options that grow exponentially over time.

Age/Stage	Description	Risk Tolerance Characteristics (Generally Speaking)	Time Horizon Characteristics
Your Early stage of work life (20s)	You're establishing work habits, personal credibility, and the ability to work well with others in the workplace.	You may be willing to risk switching jobs for better terms or be willing to relocate and work long hours.	Your focus on learning a new job is intense. Much effort is spent getting oriented to life on the job. You are likely to have plenty of evening and weekend time to spend on other career assets, especially if you are not married and if you do not have a family. For many, this is the ideal time to begin building a CareerPortfolio.
Your career-building stage (30s to mid-40s)	You're achieving momentum as a leader and decision maker. It may mean scaling back work hours to balance career and family life.	Risk tolerance in this second phase of career life depends on the personality of the individual and the options available to that individual. For most, appropriate risk taking means the ability to climb the ladder and find more opportunity.	During the early child-rearing years, it becomes critical to reevaluate which CareerPortfolio investments are most essential to achieving Personal Purpose. For some, this may mean scaling back and focusing on three out of the four areas at any given time. It may mean making occasional investments in the asset areas (such as volunteering for project once a year), not daily or weekly investments.
Your midlife stage (mid-40s to 50s)	This is when major transitions often occur and people focus on new pursuits. For some, this means a return to the workplace after raising children.	CareerPortfolio gives many in this age group the confidence to take calculated risks and make career changes.	With a Personal Purpose, putting priorities first often becomes easier as children grow older. You may find spare time more easily. Much of your efforts to prove yourself become focused on what brings you a sense of significance and purpose.

Figure 30: The CareerPortfolio and life stages (continued on page 184)

Age/Stage	Description	Risk Tolerance Characteristics (Generally Speaking)	Time Horizon Characteristics
Your latter career years (60s and, for some, 70s)	Many options exist to remain active in work and financial pursuits. Many people want to shift from work for pay to a "career" of volunteer positions. Instead of feeling compelled to retire, you can be inspired by the many choices within your reach.	Many retire from paid work and pursue a portfolio of Volunteer and Lifelong Learning activities. This age group cannot afford risk, but new pursuits are unlikely to be a threat if they're built upon a Personal Purpose. Many people continue to rely on passive forms of income generation (investments).	At this stage in life, most find it easy and enjoyable to pursue a set of activities that are meaningful.
You're 80 to 90 and still active	With technology opening convenient new ways to communicate with people around the world, your CareerPortfolio can open a whole new range of options for leading an active and productive final phase of life.	Your portfolio of time and energy investments is aligned with your Personal Purpose for this stage of life. Your activities offer rewarding, yet realistic, ways to make a difference. Risk is not part of this picture.	The variety of portfolio activities depends on the physical and mental health of the person. Because many of today's opportunities deal with information and Internet-related ways to stay connected, there should be even more opportunities for those contributing in this latter-life stage.

Figure 30: The CareerPortfolio and the Stages

Assessing your current career assets

Complete the following table to determine if your current career investments support your personal purpose.

	Meets personal purpose?	Current skills used:	Desired skills developed?
Primary			
Secondary			
Volunteer			
Lifelong Learning			

Now ask yourself the following questions:

➤ Which investments do I need to enhance or change?

➤ Which investments do I need to reduce or eliminate?

Begin thinking about the action you will need to take. You will have opportunities to map out your specific action steps.

Building Your CareerPortfolio

Develop your own personal CareerPortfolio criteria

Based on my personal purpose, my life stage, and my tolerance for risk, here are criteria by which I will begin to choose my CareerPortfolio assets.

I must be able to _____

_____

_____

(example: be a decision maker).

I must be able to _____

_____

_____

(example: be respected for my ideas).

I must be in an environment where _____

_____

_____

(example: I have a variety of work projects going on at any given time).

Skills I may need, which determine my learning investment areas:

The ability to _____

_____

_____

(example: become proficient at Web site design).

The ability to _____

_____

_____

(example: develop negotiation skills).

Goals and action plans for the year

Consider your desired CareerPortfolio. List your goals, starting with the priority CareerPortfolio area or areas you'd like to develop. For example, your goal might be to develop a Secondary Income Investment by using a hobby you now have, such as playing the piano. Your action plans might be to set your prices, determine available hours, and attract several piano students by getting the word out.

1. Goal: _____

_____

_____

Action plan(s): _____

_____

_____

By what date? _____

2. Goal: _____

_____

_____

Action plan(s): _____

_____

_____

By what date? _____

3. Goal: _____

_____

_____

Action plan(s): _____

_____

_____

By what date? _____

Personal Journal...

Life stages and time horizon

1. Using your imagination, draw your desired CareerPortfolios for the stages of life noted below. For example, you may plan a Secondary Income Source during your 40s, then choose to focus on this as your Primary Income Investment during your 50s and 60s, eliminating it altogether in your 70s.

    Label the pie charts below. For simplicity, you can write P$ for Primary Investment, S$ for Secondary Investment, V for Volunteer Investment, and L for Lifelong Learning Investments, to represent each of the career asset areas.

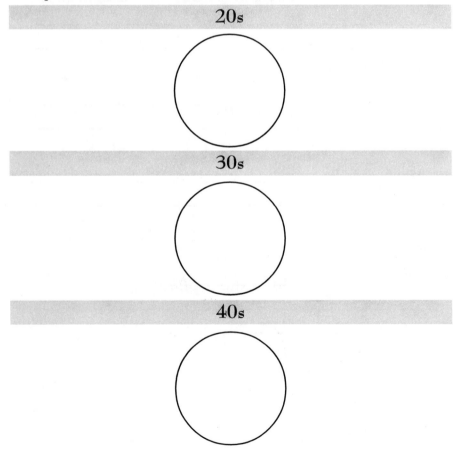

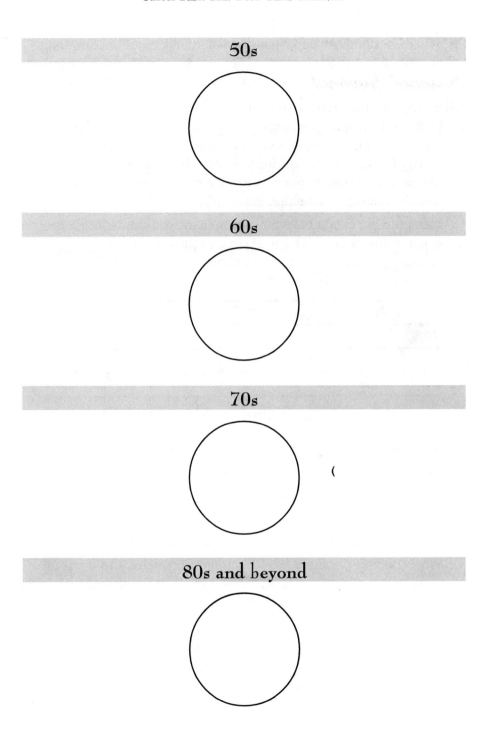

50s

60s

70s

80s and beyond

2. What are the most important, or potentially most life-altering, changes you anticipate during the decade ahead? List your anticipated changes. For example, the birth of a child, the death of a parent, a move to a new city, and so on.

_____

_____

_____

_____

_____

3. What kinds of changes will you need to consider as you deal with these events?

_____

_____

_____

_____

_____

4. How will you maintain or adapt your CareerPortfolio?

_____

_____

_____

_____

_____

5. What guiding principles will be important for you to keep in mind as you build your career during the next five years?

_____

_____

_____

_____

_____

Making time for your career investments

1. How much time per week do you think you have available to invest in career-related activities outside of your Primary Income Investment?

   _____

2. If you could find two hours for career investments each week, where would you look to find the time? Check the items that apply.

   ___ Get up earlier.

   ___ Stay up a bit later.

   ___ Find time during lunch hours.

   ___ Reduce television watching.

   ___ Delegate more at your job and leave early one day a week.

   Other: _____

   _____

   _____

3. To make time for career investments, I will spend approximately _____ hours per week. To make time, I will _____

   _____

   _____

   _____

   _____

   _____

   _____

   _____

   _____

   _____

   _____

   _____

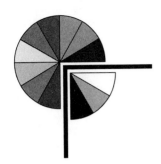

Appendix C

Taking the Right Steps Toward Your Desired CareerPortfolio

1. Draw your current CareerPortfolio diagram.

Current

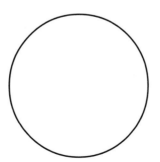

2. Determine whether the elements align with your personal purpose statement.

3. Now, draw a diagram of the CareerPortfolio that you'd like to put in place within the next 12 months.

Desired

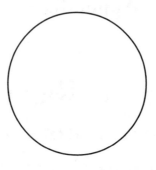

4. Note how the mix of investments differs.

5. Determine what you need to do to build your desired Career-Portfolio in the next 12 months. Be specific.

_____

_____

_____

_____

_____

_____

_____

_____

_____

_____

_____

_____

_____

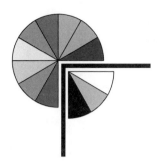

Appendix D

Internet Resources for Primary Income Investments

Here are a number of Web sites that may provide useful insight as you consider your Primary Income Investment and signs of synergy, transition, and change. They offer executive coaching, general career planning, and many additional resources.

www.ajb.dni.us

www.atb.org

www.careerbuilder.com

www.careermag.com

www.careermosaic.com

careerpath.com

www.careerresource.com

careers.wsj.com

www.coolworks.com

www.cweb.com

www.dbm.com/jobguide/intro.htm

www.getajob.com

www.gotajob.com

www.harvardpro.com/index-e.htm

isdn.net/nis

www.jobbankusa.com

jobsmart.org

www.jobweb.org

www.monster.com

www.nationjob.com

www.smartbiz.com

www.Successisfun.com

www.usajobs.opm.gov

www.Vault.com

www.Webgrrls.com

www.Wetfeet.com

www.WITI.org

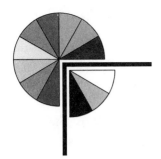

Appendix E

Secondary Income Investment Resources

Choosing a Secondary Income Investment

Here are some ideas to help you choose a Secondary Income Investment that aligns with your personal purpose and fits into your unique time constraints.

1. Brainstorm ideas that play to your strengths and to things you enjoy doing.

2. Be sure you can identify who your customer is, if you offer a product or service.

3. Be clear about the time commitment and your ability to pursue the venture.

4. The less outside financing your Secondary Income Investment needs, the more control you have and the less risk you incur. The sooner your business can support itself, the sooner it can make a profit.

5. Assess your ability to use, leverage, and grow existing skills from your Primary Income Investment.

6. Select something that you are passionate about, something you believe in.

7. Consider opportunities for earning residual income, or income that builds up over time and "works for you" even when you're not working. Examples include honest, federally registered multilevel marketing businesses that provide bonuses or commission rewards for introducing others to the business.

8. Select a Secondary Income Investment that allows you to put your first priorities first. If you have a family, you should assess your ability to schedule the project or business around your family responsibilities.

   Example: Mike, a public affairs representative, began a tax preparation business because of his wife, Mary. Mary prepared taxes from January until April, working a few hours each day while their young children were in school. Seeing Mary's success, Mike learned how to prepare taxes. While their children were young, Mary was more actively preparing clients' taxes, while Mike watched the kids. Today, their children are grown, so they've increased their tax clientele. Mike and Mary make the equivalent of Mike's Primary Income Investment within three intense months. The work, although demanding, is fun because the two can share their experiences together. Each has a separate list of clients, but they can fill in for each other in a pinch.

9. Ask yourself: "Based on my interests, hobbies, skills, education, and training, what do I like to do?" Don't open a business that you know nothing about, or pursue a field that is over-saturated.

10. If you elect to own a franchise, research the company to make sure it is stable and has the highest standards of business ethics. Be wary of any opportunity that requires large investments of any kind. I recommend that you select an opportunity that requires no debt and little or no inventory and overhead. Some home-based franchises require you to purchase a large supply of inventory. If the inventory is outdated or spoils after being on the shelf, you may get stuck with the costs.

11. You will need to address the basics of running your own business. This includes becoming familiar with bookkeeping and tax laws, as well as learning how to organize and prioritize. There are many books and professional resources that can help you address these business basics without spending a lot of money.

Secondary Income Investment Tips:

➤ Your Secondary Income Investment should support your personal purpose.

➤ Your Secondary Income Investment must be able to be integrated into your life.

➤ Start small! Take on one project at a time. Start your business while retaining your current employment.

➤ Begin gradually cultivating a contact and/or customer database before launching your business. Investigate the latest inexpensive software that can help you in customer relationship building and contact management.

➤ Reprioritize your schedule to make time for your business startup. Scaling back your schedule may be difficult at first. You will find that benchmarking all of your activities to your personal purpose and desired CareerPortfolio will help you cut out the low-priority activities.

➤ You may desire to cut back on your Primary Income Investment hours to be able to invest more time in your Secondary Income Investment. Make a commitment to leave the workplace on time at least several days a week.

> ➤ Make room financially for your Secondary Income Investment. Find ways to add financial flexibility to your life. For example, downsize existing debt and high monthly bills. When your finances are in good standing, you're better positioned to make work-related changes.

> ➤ For a more in-depth list of business startup activities in a step-by-step format, visit my Web site at *www.careerportfolio.net.*

Finding your business start-up mentors

Who might you contact to get mentoring advice on how to integrate a Secondary Income Investment into your busy schedule? List your contacts and deadlines below.

Type of advice needed	Name of contact/ mentor	By when
_____	_____	_____
_____	_____	_____
_____	_____	_____
_____	_____	_____
_____	_____	_____
_____	_____	_____
_____	_____	_____
_____	_____	_____
_____	_____	_____
_____	_____	_____
_____	_____	_____
_____	_____	_____
_____	_____	_____
_____	_____	_____

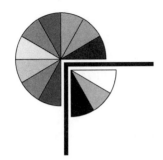

Appendix F

Volunteer Investment Resources

National Charities Information Bureau
19 Union Square West
New York, NY 10003
www.give.org

The American Institute of Philanthropy
4579 LacLede Avenue, Suite 136
St. Louis, MO 63108
www.charitywatch.org

Points of Light Foundation
1400 I Street NW, Suite 800
Washington, DC 20005
202-729-8000
www.pointsoflight.org
www.volunteerconnections.org

Web sites

www.adcouncil.org
www.bbb.org
www.impactonline.org
www.indepsec.org
www.nonprofits.org/gallery.html
www.servenet.org
www.unitedway.org

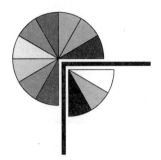

Appendix G

Lifelong Learning Resources

Use this page to record your ideas and plans for your Lifelong Learning Investment.

Focused education:

_____

_____

_____

_____

_____

_____

_____

_____

_____

_____

Focused reading:

_____

_____

_____

_____

_____

_____

_____

_____

_____

_____

_____

Mentorship (finding mentors throughout your career, and being a mentor to others):

_____

_____

_____

_____

_____

_____

_____

_____

_____

_____

_____

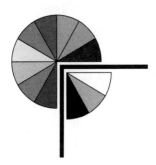

Appendix H

KidsPortfolios: CareerPortfolios for Children

This section includes ideas for helping your child develop his or her KidsPortfolio by focusing on four investments: Academics, Chores, Volunteering, and Hobbies.

Primary Investment: Academics

You can nurture your children's academic learning habits by making sure that they attend school regularly, arrive with the proper sleep and nutrition, and complete homework on time. Help them make their education their first priority. The very practice of learning will be an essential skill as we continue to move forward in a high-speed, confusing information age, where people must learn quickly and also be able to analyze complex problems.

Tips for a successful Primary Investment

➤ Set aside a place for your child to study.

➤ Check homework and have your child correct errors before turning the work in to the teacher.

➤ Attend all parent-teacher conferences. Find out how your child learns best, as well as other helpful advice to support your child's learning.

➤ Show your children how to do the job you are asking them to do.

➤ Teach them to work hard and to look for creative ways to do jobs more efficiently.

➤ Teach them to work happily.

➤ Teach them to think while they work. Ask them "why" questions ("Why do you think...?").

➤ Teach them to finish their jobs.

➤ Take your child through a mock interview for his or her first job.

Secondary Investment:
Chores, Allowance, and Responsibility

When you reward your child for work that helps the family unit, he or she develops a sense of reward for responsibility. Moreover, the child can develop entrepreneurial aptitudes if given the opportunity to decide how the money is to be spent, invested, or given to charity. For example, you can help cultivate entrepreneurial skills in your children by encouraging them to sell homemade crafts or to set up a lemonade stand (with your supervision) where interaction with customers can take place.

Often, I find that children show great enthusiasm for taking on school and civic fund-raising projects. My sons enjoy participating in school candy sales and annual fund-raising efforts. Sometimes, these fund-raisers can become a bit irritating to parents; often, I'm tempted to write a check to the school and be done with the whole thing. However, instead of considering these annual fund-raisers drudgery, I try to encourage my two sons to do their best, learning how to sell the benefits of the product at hand. By helping your child learn how to sell fund-raising products, your child can begin to build sales, negotiation, and leadership skills.

Tips for developing a Secondary Investment

➤ Help your child learn how to create things that can be sold (jewelry, lemonade, crafts, etc.).

➤ Help your children learn how to use their knowledge in a way that might someday allow them to earn extra money without disrupting their school, family, and other commitments. Examples might include tutoring a younger child in reading, teaching art in summer camp, and so on.

➤ Teach your children how to do their own laundry, iron their shirts, and shine their shoes in order to complete important jobs that go beyond homework. Reward responsibility with a small allowance. Open a savings account. Have them save a certain sum of money that you agree to match once they meet their goals.

➤ Purchase a complicated model and set a time limit to have it done. This can reinforce the importance of completing a project outside of school work.

➤ Have an accomplished musician or athlete talk with your children about endurance. This fosters a stick-to-it attitude outside of core school work.

➤ Visit a fire department and ask one of the firefighters to discuss courage and risk taking.

Volunteer Investment

Caring about other people can start at a young age. Through serving others, children learn how to be contributing members of the human community. Beyond good citizenship, children can learn cooperation, tolerance, loyalty, and respect for life. According to a 1994 Gallup poll sponsored by Family Matters, a program of the Points of Light Foundation in Washington, D.C., when people start volunteering as young children, they are likely to become lifelong volunteers.

Although not all volunteer activities are appropriate for preschoolers and young children, with a bit of research, you can find creative ways to involve your child in organizations and causes that welcome participation from the whole family.

Tips for the Volunteer Investment

➤ Help your child use his or her knowledge to assist worthwhile causes that are aligned with your child's personal purpose. For example, if your child enjoys writing, he or she could help a nonprofit organization write thank-you notes, either by hand or on a computer.

➤ To make family volunteering a rewarding experience for young children, you can talk about a specific issue and discuss what you as a family have a responsibility to do. Ask your children how your family can help.

➤ For children, volunteer projects should be as hands-on as possible. If you and your child prepare food for the homeless and bring it to a shelter, it will be far more meaningful than if you were to write a check and mail it.

➤ Once you've completed a volunteer activity, reflect on what you've learned. You can ask questions that allow your children to express their feelings about the volunteer experience. You could also have them draw pictures of the experience and display them around your home to reaffirm their contributions. If your child gives a can of food to a food drive, you could ask your child to write a few paragraphs describing how the food will help another family. Or perhaps your child could tell an imaginary story about who receives the food and how the donation makes a difference. This makes the project much more real to the child.

➤ Whatever volunteer activity you choose to do with your youngster, never force a child who is resistant. You can eliminate any fear by explaining in simple terms why a volunteer project is important and by reminding the child that you'll be right there with him or her.

Lifelong Learning Investment: Hobbies

Hobbies require an extra amount of energy and commitment from parents. That's because getting good at a hobby, such as playing the piano, requires lots of encouragement and parental involvement.

Tips for the Lifelong Learning Investment:

You can help your child develop learning skills beyond the classroom environment.

Here are a few ideas:

> ➤ Help your child discover a hobby simply by asking what interests him or her.

> ➤ Once you've received input from your child, begin to talk with other parents and investigate resources for discovering the best teachers or learning environments for that hobby.

> ➤ Teach your child how to use such reference resources as the Internet, public libraries, and newspapers.

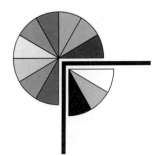

Appendix I

Business Startup Checklist

___ Before startup, determine your market (or potential market). Define the characteristics of your market. If there are a number of target markets or audiences, describe each one in detail—including age, location, and why these people would want to buy your products or services.

___ If you are not sure about going full-scale into a business, try your skills on a very small and informal scale with a few customers. Be sure to produce documented billing statements for tax purposes.

___ If you're ready to establish a business and see the business grow, choose management advisers (or trusted business mentors) who have proven business credibility and success. You should include a banker, an accountant, and an attorney.

___ Develop, or get some help developing, a business plan. Be sure to include cash flow projections.

___ Take the business plan to your banker for review. Possible needed bank services could include:

1. Credit card merchant account.

2. Business checking account.

3. Working capital loan.

4. Equipment loan.

5. Lock-box services.

___ Decide which type of legal entity (corporation, sole proprietorship, partnership, etc.) your business will be and select the fiscal year end. Here are some of the legal documents that you may need:

1. Partnership agreements.

2. Articles of incorporation and first organizational minutes.

3. Bylaws.

4. Federal identification number (SS-4).

5. State and local license applications.

6. Sales tax identification number.

7. State unemployment number.

8. Any trade or industry licenses.

___ Get another phone number if needed, and order office supplies, business cards, and stationery.

___ Select a financial record keeping and billing system. You'll need to allow for accounts payable, accounts receivable, inventory tracking, order entry, and contact management (keeping records on whom you've worked with, spoken to, or otherwise interacted with). You can work with a certified public accountant or bookkeeper to outsource the setup, or you can gain advice from those who can help you streamline the process.

___ Purchase adequate insurance, if necessary.

___ Determine a location for your business (home, rented office, etc.). If necessary, negotiate a lease.

___ Design the layout of your office space, if applicable.

___ In addition to the business plan, establish a marketing plan that defines your product, price, place of business, methods of promotion, and so on.

___ Promote the business by using the promotion tools that are most relevant: public relations (press releases with reporter follow-up), advertising, direct mail to targeted audiences, coupons, special discounts, trade shows, and other face-to-face communication venues, including special events and in-store promotions.

___ Hire employees, if relevant. A recruitment or search firm can be helpful, depending on your business needs.

___ Other ongoing operational functions include personnel policies and procedures, tax filings, financial audits (an internal review), payroll operations, and business procedures to add quality control and consistency.

These are some of the major startup activities. Your business is unique, and not all of these activities may apply.

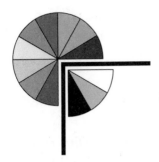

Bibliography

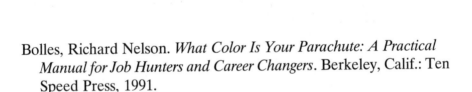

Bolles, Richard Nelson. *What Color Is Your Parachute: A Practical Manual for Job Hunters and Career Changers*. Berkeley, Calif.: Ten Speed Press, 1991.

Cleaver, Joanne. "How to Profit From Volunteering." *Parents*, July 1998.

Covey, Stephen, R. *The Seven Habits of Highly Effective People*. New York: Fireside, 1989.

Fisher, Roger, and William Ury. *Getting to Yes: Negotiating Agreement Without Giving In*. New York: Penguin Books, 1991.

Hammer, Michael. *Beyond Re-Engineering: How the Process-Centered Organization Is Changing Our Work and Our Lives*. New York: HarperBusiness, 1996.

Kleiman, Carol. "The Right Reasons for a Job Change." Tribune Media Services WebPoint, *www.webpoint.com*.

Larson, Jane. "Find Success, Freedom: 'Micropreneur' Says Home Business the Way." *The Arizona Republic,* 22 July 1998.

LeBoeuf, Michael. *The Perfect Business: How to Make a Million From Home.* New York: Fireside, 1998.

Whitford, David. "Confessions of an Online Moonlighter." *Fortune,* 27 April 1998, 443.

Worzel, Richard. *From Employee to Entrepreneur: How to Turn Your Experience Into a Fortune*. Toronto, Ontario, Canada: Key Porter Books, 1989.

Sinetar, Marsha. *The Mentor's Spirit: Life Lessons on Leadership and the Art of Encouragement.* New York: St. Martin's Press, 1998.

Hutchins, David B. "Mentoring." *SHRM White Paper*, 20 July, 1997.

Sullivan, Robert. *The Small Business Start-Up Guide.* Niantic, Conn.: The Business Book Press, 1998.

Kimmel, Tim. *Raising Kids Who Turn Out Right.* Phoenix, Ariz.: Generation Ministries, 1998.

Spaide, Deborah. *Teaching Your Kids to Care: How to Discover and Develop the Spirit of Charity in Your Children*. Secaucus, N.J.: Carol Publishing Group, 1997.

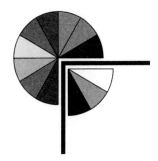

Index

About the Author...

Carol A. Poore is passionate about living each day with purpose. To live purposefully and to help others find their special purpose is what drives Carol to share the CareerPortfolio concept with others who want to live and work in a meaningful way.

A native Arizonan, Carol is a published author, speaker, and community leader based in Phoenix. Her career includes directing the marketing and communication operations of New West Energy, a major energy service provider in the southwestern United States. Her CareerPortfolio includes expertise in executive leadership, strategic planning, marketing, campaign management, and communication strategy development. With a master's degree in business administration and a bachelor's degree in broadcasting and journalism, Carol has pioneered several business startup ventures and has been in the corporate trenches as an executive, employee, and entrepreneur. She is an accredited business communicator through the International Association of Business Communicators (IABC).

As a volunteer, Carol has lent her leadership skills to the Arizona-based Fiesta Bowl Football Championship Games and Events, Valley Leadership, the International Association of Business Communicators, Super Bowl XXX, Parents Anonymous of Arizona, and the Arrowhead Community Bank Board of Directors. She also serves on the Board of Directors of the Arizona Retailers' Association. As a wife and mother, Carol emphasizes CareerPortfolios that promote a balanced work and family life.

For speaking engagements, contact:
Carol A. Poore
E-mail: *cp@careerportfolio.net*
Fax: (602) 274-4709